P9-APO-928

Penmanship

for Christian Writing

Penmanship

for Christian Writing

Grade 1

Teacher's Manual

Rod and Staff Publishers, Inc.
P.O. Box 3, Hwy. 172
Crockett, Kentucky 41413
Telephone: (606) 522-4348

Acknowledgements

We acknowledge that our omniscient, ever-present Lord has provided us the opportunity and understanding for a venture of this sort. Working closely together, those involved have been enabled by God to establish this new Penmanship series. Our desire has been to please the Lord in providing this course for the Christian school.

We also acknowledge that we have benefited from other handwriting systems in developing the system used in this series. And many teachers were also consulted.

Research and Writing—Daniel Strubhar
Final Editing—Marvin Eicher
Artwork—Daniel Zook; Lester Miller

Grade One Curriculum

Pupil's Workbook Units 1, 2
Pupil's Workbook Units 3, 4
Pupil's Workbook Unit 5
Teacher's Manual

Copyright, 1988

By Rod and Staff Publishers, Inc.
Crockett, Kentucky 41413

Printed in U.S.A.

ISBN 978-07399-0559-3
Catalog no. 15191

Table of Contents

Introduction
to Penmanship Series

Penmanship is a subject that many teachers have often overlooked. The reasons are many and varied; but no doubt the main reason is simply that other subjects are considered to be more important, and penmanship has been crowded into the background. But we feel that handwriting needs to hold a prominent place in our Christian school curriculums and that it needs to be taught in an orderly, thorough, and efficient manner. This is the basic reason behind the production of this handwriting series.

The Importance of Teaching Penmanship in Our Schools

1. Good penmanship is a mark of Christian carefulness. God expects His people to be thorough and exact in their activities, not slipshod and careless.

2. Good penmanship is a mark of Christian courtesy. Writing that is difficult to read will not be appreciated by those who must read it.

3. Good penmanship is necessary for good communication. Even though word processors and copiers have taken over in many areas of communication, there are still many purposes for writing that are better accomplished by means of handwriting.

4. Good penmanship is an aid to efficiency. Well-written messages are far less time-consuming to read than those poorly written.

5. Good penmanship will affect students' attitudes. If neat writing is insisted upon, the very act of penning words and sentences in a neat manner will cause students to want to do their best work.

6. Good penmanship on the part of our students will leave a good testimony for our school program. Penmanship is the first thing that impresses the critical eye, before the quality of the work done is apparent.

7. We need to teach good penmanship because it is right. We must do well whatever needs to be done. "Whatsoever thy hand findeth to do, do it with thy might" (Ecclesiastes 9:10).

Our Approach to Handwriting

1. Teaching by Strokes

Teaching handwriting by strokes is the simplest and most efficient way to get the principles of handwriting across. With this approach, the child learns and practices a few basic strokes from which most letters are composed. As he learns these strokes, he has a tool for conquering difficulties in letter formation. In practicing the strokes, he will also become better acquainted with the feel of the basic movements of handwriting, which will help his handwriting to become more efficient and more automatic.

The stroke approach is also beneficial from the teacher's standpoint. It gives him something to teach in handwriting, rather than allowing handwriting instruction to degenerate into nothing more than remedial work. It tends to give a greater enthusiasm for handwriting, because the teacher will know better how to teach it.

Here is how two typical letters are learned by the stroke method:

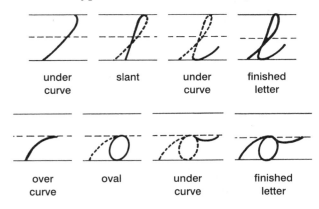

| under curve | slant | under curve | finished letter |

| over curve | oval | under curve | finished letter |

2. Teaching Quality

In this course we want to give considerable attention to the teaching of quality. Quality includes slant, alignment, size, proportion, line quality, and spacing, and is a very important part of handwriting (see diagrams and definitions below). The proper teaching of quality may spell the difference between success and failure in teaching handwriting. The teaching of quality should not be too far removed from the teaching of letter form, so that the children do not separate the two in everyday writing.

7

Definitions:

    Slant—degree to which a letter is slanted

        consistent slant—all letters slanted the same

        correct slant—straight up and down for first grade manuscript; leaning forward for slant print and cursive

    Alignment—tops and bottoms of letters in straight lines

    Size—largeness or smallness of letters in comparison with what they should be (guidelines for size are specific in each grade)

    Proportion—size of letters or letter parts in relation to other letters or letter parts

    Line quality—degree of lightness or heaviness of writing, related to pencil pressure

    Spacing—distance between words, letters, or sentences

Diagrams of the six areas of quality:

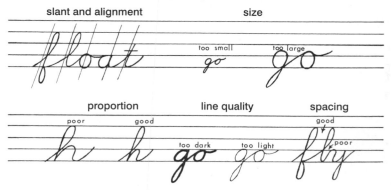

3. Difference in Emphasis at Various Grade Levels

In this course, we follow an emphasis at each grade level that builds upon the previous grade, while also reviewing a large part of the previous year's material. The first three grades contain the bulk of new material. For this reason, these grades are the most basic, and the teachers of these grades must be especially careful to give the children a right foundation in handwriting. Grade four contains the least new material.

Quality should receive a greater emphasis in grades four to six, and the teachers of these three grades must put forth a continual effort to keep the students' handwriting up to the standard. In seventh and eighth grades, teachers must emphasize speed, efficiency, and practical handwriting applications in everyday life, while still continuing an emphasis on handwriting quality.

8

Posture, Pencil Holding, and Paper Placement

Following are standards for proper posture, pencil holding, and paper placement:

1. Posture at seat
   a. Sit back in the seat.
   b. Sit up straight
   c. Have feet flat on the floor.
   d. Lean slightly forward from the hips.
   e. Have one arm on desk, holding paper, while the other arm writes.

POSTURE

Sit and stand with your back straight and with both feet flat on the floor. Lean forward only a little when you sit at your desk.

2. Posture at blackboard
   a. Stand squarely on both feet directly in front of the blackboard.
   b. Stand back six to twelve inches from the blackboard.

3. Pencil holding
   a. Pencil should be held between the thumb and first finger, resting lightly on the second finger.
   b. Pencil should be held no more firmly than necessary for control.
   c. Pencil must not be cramped or pinched.
4. Chalk holding
   a. Chalk should be held firmly between thumb and first two fingers.
   b. Chalk should point toward the palm of the hand and be perpendicular to the blackboard.

 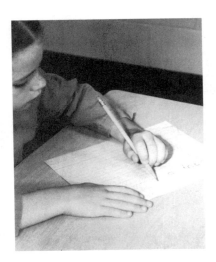

PENCIL HOLDING

Hold the pencil so that its top points back over your shoulder. Hold it tightly enough to control it, but do not pinch it.

5. Paper placement
   a. For manuscript writing, paper should always be placed straight up and down on the desk top, except that left-handers should slant it to the right. For cursive writing, right-handers should slant the paper about thirty degrees to the left, and left-handers should slant it toward the right as taught in "Special instructions for Left-handed Pupils."

b. The paper should be on the side of the desk toward the arm that will be used to write.

PAPER PLACEMENT

If you write with your right hand, place the paper straight in front of you. If you write with your left hand, slant the top of the paper to the right.

Special Instructions
for Left-handed Pupils

Many teachers seem confused when it comes to teaching left-handed pupils how to write. How should they slant their papers and hold their pencils? How can they write so as to be able to see their writing? How does one prevent them from developing a hooked wrist? This section is intended to answer these questions with sound, positive directions for teachers of left-handers. Although some points may seem strange and even impractical, note carefully that *these principles were developed over several decades* of experimentation with left-handers in many schools. Those left-handers who learned to write by this method developed a neater, more even, and more efficient handwriting style than those taught by other methods. Therefore, unless your left-handed students have already formed poor writing habits, these principles will practically guarantee success if you diligently follow them.

A left-handed pupil must deal with a peculiar handicap when he learns to write. Writing moves from left to right; and for the left-handed person this means that his writing hand will cover his writing as he moves long. Therefore, many left-handers resort to what seems the simplest solution: a hooked wrist.

However, the hooked wrist is by no means the best solution to this problem. This method makes writing laboriously slow, inefficient, and unpleasant. A far better method is to teach left-handed pupils *from the start* that there are certain things they must do differently than right-handed pupils if they are to write well. These differences are listed here.

1. Instead of placing their papers vertically (or slanted to the left for cursive) on their desks, *left-handers must always slant their papers to the right*. In first grade their arms should meet the lines of their papers at right angles; later, *for cursive writing*, their arms should meet their papers *across the lower right-hand corner*. Although this much slant may seem extreme, experience has shown that this is the best way for left-handers to get the proper slant on their letters without using a hooked wrist.

2. *Left-handers should always write toward, not away from, themselves*. If they slant their papers properly, as outlined in number 1 above, they will naturally do this. But when they

write at the blackboard, you will need to make special provisions so that this is possible. *Therefore, give a left-handed child about twice as much room at the blackboard* as what you give to a right-handed child. Then, instead of writing in the space directly in front of him, he can start in the space to his left and write *toward himself* as a left-handed writer should.

3. *Left-handers should hold their pencils exactly the same way that right-handers do.* If they cannot see their writing, either they are holding the pencil too close to the point or their desks are too high. Left-handers can normally write better at a desk lower than usual, because they can better see over their writing hand that way.

4. *If you have a large number of left-handers, group them together* for penmanship classes if possible. This would be especially good in the lower grades, where handwriting habits are first being established. In this way they will not become confused as easily by the right-handers, and you can more quickly see whether they are developing proper habits. Place this group to the right side of the class (as you face the front) so that they can read, as well as write, *toward themselves.*

5. In slant printing and cursive writing, the left-hander's strokes are opposite of the right hander's. The right-hander *pulls* downstrokes vertically *toward himself,* whereas the left-hander should *push* downstrokes horizontally *away from himself.* Also, the right-hander *pushes* across strokes horizontally *away from himself,* but the left-hander should *pull* across strokes vertically *toward himself.* Study this diagram carefully:

Left-hander	**Right-hander**
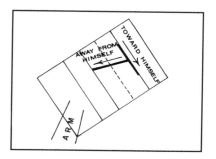	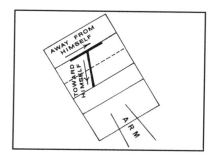

Again, do not be surprised if you have never heard of some of these points. Perhaps *your* teachers never heard of them either! Begin *now* to put them to use—and do so by all means if you are a first or second grade teacher. Then you will have the satisfaction of teaching by a definite method that works, and you will have begun on the road to successful handwriting for your left-handed pupils.

Illustrations for proper pencil holding, paper placement, and writing method for left-handed pupils are included in the section "Posture, Pencil Holding, and Paper Placement."

How to Treat the Teacher's Manual

In this course there is a detailed teacher's manual for each lesson. The teacher's manual gives direction to the teacher on what goals to strive for, how to fill out the workbooks, and how to conduct the class so that the children gain the clearest possible understanding of the lesson. It also gives other diagnostic, remedial, and informative suggestions. And each lesson in the teacher's manual has a reduction of the student workbook lesson, for your handy reference.

We suggest that you as a teacher do not overlook the daily teacher's manual in your preparation for class but that you study it carefully sometime previous to the class period. Especially the inexperienced teacher should read over it carefully and thoroughly, paying special attention to the section entitled "Conducting the Class." Do not let your teaching flounder because of a lack of understanding of the subject material and correct class procedure. Even an experienced teacher does well to study the teacher's manual, although he may already be able to teach the writing of the alphabet successfully. It will help him to understand the approach we are taking in the teaching of this course, and the sequence of thought throughout the lessons.

We suggest not only that you read the manual for each lesson a few hours previous to teaching it but also that you read ahead in the teacher's manual from time to time, to keep abreast of just where you are in accomplishing your goals for the year. You may also find that some of the suggestions that are given in future lessons may be helpful to you in the lessons you are presently teaching, even though they may not always be directly applicable to the present lesson.

Do not take for granted that just because something is not mentioned in the teacher's manual for a particular lesson, it is therefore not to be considered in that lesson. For example, not every lesson mentions that you should be sure your children practice correct posture and pencil-holding habits, but you should watch for this each day. Various items of this nature will be brought to your attention from time to time as reminders to keep watching these areas.

Finally, do not be a slave to your teacher's manual. You do not have to accept every suggestion or follow the exact procedure for every class period that is outlined, right down to saying the exact words that are suggested. The teacher's manual is there to guide the teacher's thinking and is not the final rule of procedure for every situation. However, the basic suggestions were included because they were felt to be important, and the teacher should consider and use them in one form or another as he plans the lesson

To the First Grade Teacher

First grade is one of the most important grades in school because it lays the foundation for the remainder of the child's school experience. If the foundation is laid as it should be, the learning structure is not nearly as likely to fail. Here are several things that are important blocks in the first grade foundation:

1. *A good teacher example.* How well do *you* print manuscript? Are you careless? Your students might become lost if you do not have good writing habits. Check yourself and improve as necessary.
2. *A thorough learning of each letter.* You will fail in this if you let the mediocre pass as good enough. Make sure each child is forming each letter correctly from the start.
3. *Correct habits of posture, pencil holding, and paper placement.* Encourage beginning with right habits in these areas and continuing in them.
4. *Not allowing significantly poorer work in daily assignments than in the writing lesson.* The child should understand that what he learns in penmanship class must be applied in other subjects. This would apply especially in the latter part of the year once the child has learned to write words and sentences.

Course Organization and Goals

The course includes 150 lessons and is organized into five units, not all of equal length. Each unit has a title that relates to the material included in that unit and builds upon the previous one. Unit 1 begins with the basic strokes that make up the letters, Unit 2 moves on into small letters and numerals, Unit 3 teaches how to form words and properly space the letters, Unit 4 teaches capital letters, and Unit 5 gives practice in writing sentences.

The major goal for the first grade is *By the end of the year the children should have manuscript writing and numerals well established both in theory and in practice.* The children should also know—

1. how letters are composed of strokes;
2. how to write their names;
3. how to write words in sentences and space correctly between them;
4. how to write letters in proper proportion and at the proper height.

Time Spent in Writing Class

The course is designed for approximately one lesson each day. One hundred fifty lessons allows thirty extra days in case the class is missed at times or in case some lessons require more than one day for mastery. The teacher should allow fifteen to thirty minutes for the first grade writing class. Depending upon your class, it may take more time.

Conducting the Class Period

In teaching a letter of the alphabet, follow this procedure:

1. *Explain the formation of the letter by strokes on the blackboard.* The blackboard is an aid because a child can both see and hear the explanation at the same time.
2. *The children should practice the letter themselves immediately following the blackboard demonstration,* both on the blackboard and on paper. Blackboard practice helps a child in beginning writing because it is normally difficult for a first grader to coordinate his muscles for small writing.
3. *Have the children work the lesson,* supervising their work. Do not allow them to do the lesson on their own, or they will form poor writing habits. As soon as you discover a child doing something incorrectly, show him what he is doing wrong and how to do it right. If you discover that a large number in the class are making the same mistake, call the attention of the whole class to the problem and use the blackboard for further explanation.
4. *Have the children practice some more on other paper after* they have finished their lessons, *if* you are not sure that the material has been well learned. (The reverse side of most lessons may be used for extra practice.) Their work should be satisfactory to you before you go on. Naturally, do not expect perfection immediately.

What Kind of Work Should You Expect?

Do not expect a first grader to write a perfect letter the very first time, with perfectly straight lines and well-rounded curves. However, you can expect that once the child has learned how the letter is to be made, he should be able to form the letter thereafter correctly according to the basic strokes, even though imperfectly made. You should expect the child to have improved the general appearance of his letters by the time he begins writing words and sentences. By the end of the year, the child should be able to make each manuscript letter with straight lines, nicely rounded curves, proper proportion, and proper height. However, if at *any* point there is *great* deviation from the standard letter, the child should correct it.

Left-handed Pupils

The first grade teacher needs to observe shortly after the beginning of school which children are naturally left-handed and which are naturally right-handed. This can generally be done simply by noticing with which hand they pick up the pencil to use it. Many times they may already have been trained at home to use either the left or right hand with a pencil, based on the parents' observation. You may want to talk with the parents of the child if you are undecided.

You will need to pay special attention to the left-handed pupil in order to insure that he forms correct habits. Study carefully the section "Special Instructions for Left-handed Pupils."

Evaluation and Grading

Evaluation involves looking over the child's paper for errors in form, neatness, quality, and so forth. In doing this, you should make notations on the child's paper, showing him exactly what is wrong with his work, so that he knows why he got the number of errors he did and how to improve.

You probably will not want to take a grade on every lesson in first grade writing. The reason is that when the child is learning something for the first time in his life, it is not fair to him to make his first try count as very important in his final grade. It is better to grade his second try or later.

Both in evaluating (which you should do to every lesson) and in grading, you want to consider the number and importance of the errors. Errors in form are the most important and must count the most in a grade. Errors of quality, such as spacing and alignment, come next in importance. Negligent errors and lack of smoothness or evenness would be the least important, although they should also have attention called to them. Factors such as neatness and the class's progress in learning up to that point need to be considered too. Do not give just one glance at a paper and then slap a grade on it from first impression. Grade on the basis of specific errors.

You will also need to set in your own mind just what will constitute a perfect or a failing paper. It is difficult to make a sample of just what is expected from a first grader, though some have no doubt tried. There are too many styles of good and poor writing. One guideline, though, may be this: Do not fall into the habit of giving an *A-* for a poor paper, an *A* for an average paper, and an *A+* for an excellent paper. Make your grades mean something. If your children's grades are all in the very high or the very low bracket, something may be wrong with your grading system.

Miscellaneous Helps

1. It is very important that proper standards of posture, pencil holding, and paper placement be established right from the beginning. Expect to have some difficulty particularly with pencil holding at first. Children will want to hold the pencil in whatever way seems easiest for them but which will not likely be the best way to learn to write.

2. *Special, large beginning pencils* are sometimes used for beginning writers. Keep some on hand if necessary for the child who has real difficulty using the regular pencils. *Do not use them unless needed,* since it may make learning to hold a regular pencil difficult.

3. *Do not make the pencil point too sharp.* For the beginning writer who is unsure of himself and has large spaces to write in, a dull pencil makes a better line. It will also be easier for the child to learn to make neat letters if the point of the pencil is dull.

4. Student pages are perforated, and we suggest they be torn out of their books prior to use. Tearing out the pages and placing them flat on the desk will make writing easier for the children.

5. Remember to *use the extra practice paper on the back of each lesson page throughout the book.* Do not hesitate to do this, because plenty of practice is a must.

6. If you would like to use more paper than what is in the book, *get special first grade writing paper* that is *similar to the pattern used in this course* (available from Rod and Staff Publishers). If for some reason the child must use tablet paper, he should write two spaces high for tall letters and one space high for short letters. He should move ahead four lines for each new row. You

may want to mark in advance the lines on his paper where he is to write.

7. *Lines drawn on the blackboard* for blackboard practice should be the proper distance apart, possibly 2 1/2 *inches between lines.* One of the best and easiest ways to draw the lines is to *use a music scorer, removing the second and fourth chalks. Some also use a felt-tip marking pen* to draw semi-permanent lines on the blackboard the correct distance apart and at the right height. The lines will eventually wear off, but they are more conven-ient in that they do not have to be relined each time.

8. Remember to *place the lines on the blackboard at the correct height* for the children. The lines should be just slightly below eye level, which will of course vary with different grades and ages.

Unit 1

The Basic Manuscript Strokes

Lessons 1–9

Lesson 1
Making Straight Lines

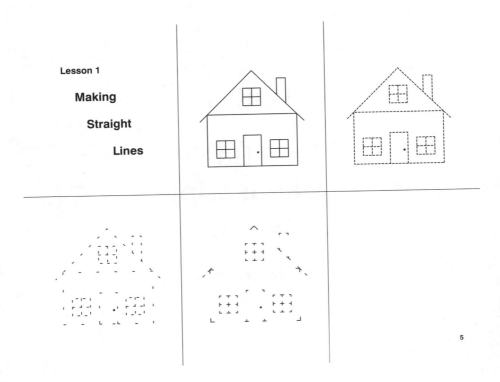

Lesson 1

Making

Straight

Lines

5

Aim of the Lesson

To help the teacher evaluate the children's abilities and coordination in drawing straight lines; to give the child a frame of reference to begin making straight lines.

Directions

The children are to trace over the four houses shown and then draw one of their own in the blank space.

Conducting the Class

Be sure the children are **sitting up straight on their seats** with their **feet on the floor.**

Hand out their writing books to them.

Give them pencils and **show them how they are to be held.** (See "Posture, Pencil Holding, and Paper Placement.")

As they tear out the first lesson, **explain that in order to write well, we need to know how to make straight lines.**

Ask the children:

"What do you see on this page?" (Houses.)

"What do you do in a house?" (Eat, sleep, work, sing, pray, and suchlike.)

"What is wrong with most of the houses on this page?" (There are empty spaces in the lines that make up the frame.)

Tell the children to **take their pencils.** First they trace over the house with solid lines and then **fill in the empty spaces** in the walls, roofs, chimneys, windows, and doors by drawing lines over them. They shall make the **lines as straight as they can** (without a ruler). When they are finished, they should **draw their own house** in the empty space as accurately as possible. The house they draw should look very much like the others.

Further Helps for the Teacher

Be very particular right from the beginning **about** your children's **posture and pencil-holding habits.** Watch the children as they are working, and correct any improper habits in either of these areas.

As the children draw over their houses, you will probably need to **help them understand just where to put the lines,** especially on the less detailed houses.

If you have the children do any drawing on the blackboard, **show them how to follow the rules for blackboard writing.** (See "Posture, Pencil holding, and Paper Placement.")

Check over the children's work carefully when they are finished. **By observing** how uniformly, accurately, and straight the lines are drawn, **you may be able to get a good idea about the kind of problems you will face later** in teaching strokes and letters.

Lesson 2
Lines That Go Down

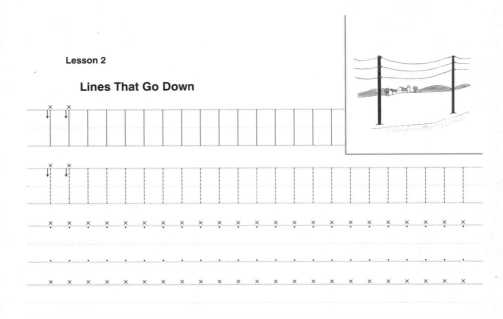

Aim of the Lesson

To teach the vertical manuscript stroke.

Directions

The children should trace over the solid and dotted lines in the first two rows and draw lines between the dots in the third row. The fourth row is for more practice. Each stroke is to be begun at the x for proper spacing.

Conducting the Class

Explain to the children that different kinds of lines are used to make letters. **The down line is one kind** that is used to make letters. After they learn the different kinds of lines, they will learn to make letters with them.

Ask the children if they can think of anything that runs up and down like the lines on this page. After they have given their suggestions, talk about the picture (telephone poles) in the upper corner of the page.

After **demonstrating the down line on the board,** check to see that all the children are **sitting up straight** and **holding their pencils correctly.** As they **trace, they should try to stay exactly on the lines. Have them retrace the lines several times** to get the feel of the downstroke.

On the third row, tell the children to **aim carefully for the bottom dot** when they start from the top dot so that they do not have a crooked line.

In the fourth row, **watch that their lines do not become slanted** but remain vertical.

Further Helps for the Teacher

The purpose of the picture in each lesson is to help the child **establish a relationship between the picture and the stroke** he is learning. You can use the pictures to help the child to remember the strokes if he forgets them later on.

Be sure that your children **start at the top** (the x) and go down, not vice versa.

Blackboard practice would be helpful in this lesson, especially for slower children.

Lesson 3

Lines That Go Across

Lesson 3

Lines That Go Across

x→ — x→ — —— —— x→-- x→-- ----- -----

x→ — x→ — —— —— x→-- x→-- ----- -----

x· · x· · x· · x· · x· · x· · x· · x· · x· · x· ·

x· · x· · x· · x· · x· · x· · x· · x· · x· · x· ·

x x x x x x x x x x x

x x x x x x x x x x x

Review

x x
↓ ↓

9

Aim of the Lesson

To teach the horizontal manuscript stroke.

Directions

Have the children trace over the solid and dotted lines in the first row and draw lines between the dots in the second row. The third row is for practice. They should begin each line at the *x* and make it approximately the same length as the lines in the other rows. The fourth row is review for the vertical stroke of the previous lesson.

28

Conducting the Class

Ask the children:

"What kind of line did you study in the last lesson?" (They should be able to tell you readily if the lesson was well learned.)

"What do you see in the picture in the corner of this page?" (A ladder.)

"Can you think of anything else that has lines running across?" (You should have some things in mind in case they cannot think of any!)

Demonstrate the horizontal stroke on the board, explaining that it is simply a straight line that goes sideways across the page rather than up and down. Be sure they understand which side they are to begin on when making this line.

Once the children are ready to write, **remind them of their posture** and **of the way they are to hold their pencils.** Again, **check to see if they are staying on the lines** as they trace and retrace over them. Be on hand to **observe them** as they work.

On the second row, be sure the children understand that **they are to draw lines** *across* from dot to dot, *not* down from dot to dot.

Further Helps for the Teacher

Pay special attention to the review line. The review line is a new feature of this lesson but will continue to be a part of many of the lessons. **A good pattern of review is essential** to help the child retain what he has learned. The child may have a **tendency to forget how a previous stoke or letter was made,** or he **may simply become careless** in doing work that he has done well before. Both need to be watched for and corrected each time the review line is worked.

If you prefer, you may have the children **do their review line before they work on the new stroke.** In some cases this may help to tie the old lesson to the new more effectively.

Lesson 4
Lines That Slant Backward

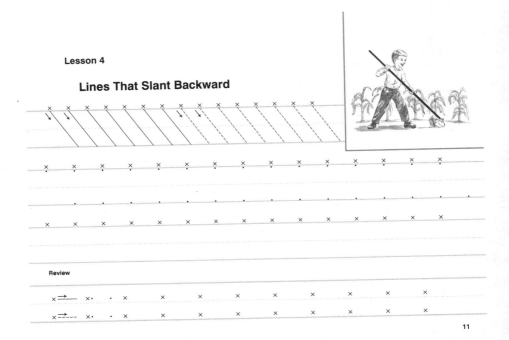

Lesson 4

Lines That Slant Backward

Review

11

Aim of the Lesson

To teach the backward-slanting manuscript stroke.

Directions

The children should trace over the solid and dotted lines in the first row. In row two, slanted lines are to be drawn between the dots, beginning each stroke at the x. In row three, slanted lines are also to be drawn, beginning each stroke at the x. Row four is a review of the horizontal stroke. Horizontal lines are to be drawn, beginning each stroke at the x.

Conducting the Class

Ask the children:

"What is this little boy doing?" (Hoeing.)

"How many of you have helped your parents by doing what this boy is doing?"

"What does the boy have that looks a little like the lines on this page?" (A hoe.)

Explain to the children that this line does not run either straight up and down or straight across, as do the lines in the previous two lessons. **Instead, it** *slants*. **It slants backward,** so we call it a **backward-slanting line.** It begins at the top line and slants until it reaches the bottom line. This line also is used to make letters.

When you are sure the children understand backward-slanting lines (see "Further Helps for the Teacher"), **proceed** with the lesson as usual, **checking posture and pencil holding** and giving **careful supervision and help** as needed.

Further Helps for the Teacher

In this lesson, be sure your children understand—

1. How a **backward-slanting line differs from a vertical or horizontal line;**
2. that it is **one of the kinds of lines** that make up letters;
3. **how to make a backward-slanting line** that looks right.

Sometime in today's lesson, you will want to **tie Lessons 2–4 together** in the children's minds by helping them remember that these different kinds of lines they are learning are all used to make letters. If some want to learn to make the letters immediately, help them realize that to do their best in making letters, they need to learn to make the different kinds of lines first. **Keep their enthusiasm up** by telling them that if they learn how to make the lines well, they will start learning the letters in a few days.

The **slanting lines will be more difficult** for the children to make than the horizontal and vertical lines. The child will probably have **trouble getting the slant at the right angle.** This is something that will come with practice, so give them plenty of it. You may want to get out some extra paper for them to practice on until they can do well enough to satisfy you.

Also, **some children may get this stroke mixed up with the**

forward-slanting or slant-to-the-right stroke. We do want to strictly differentiate between these strokes so that the child gets the proper term associated with the proper stroke. This will help in teaching letters with these strokes later.

Some **blackboard practice would be helpful** in this lesson. Not only will it be easier for them because of the larger motions, but also it will be easier for you to see just how each child is doing and to give corrections when necessary.

Lesson 5
Lines That Slant Forward

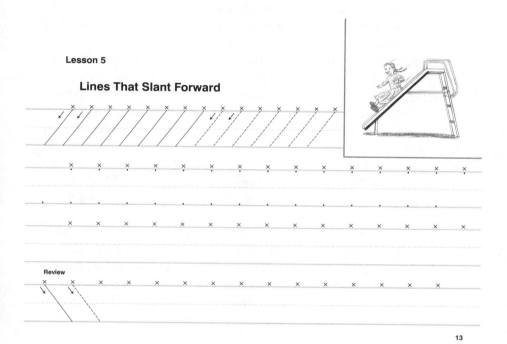

Lesson 5

Lines That Slant Forward

Review

13

Aim of the Lesson

To teach the forward-slanting manuscript stroke.

Directions

The children should trace over the solid and dotted lines in the first row. In row two, forward-slanting lines should be drawn between the dots, beginning each stroke at the x. In row three, forward-slanting lines again should be drawn, beginning each stroke at the x. Row four is a review of the backward-slanting line. Backward-slanting lines are to be draw, beginning each stroke at the x.

Conducting the Class

Ask the children:

"What do you see in the picture at the top of the page that looks like the lines on this page?" (A sliding board.)

"What is the difference between this line and the line we drew in the last lesson?" (This line slants forward rather than backward.)

Explain to the children that **we call this line a forward-slanting line.** In the last lesson, we drew backward-slanting lines. A forward-slanting line **leans just the opposite direction** from a backward-slanting line. **We do start at the top** to make it, just the same as a backward-slanting line, but it slants the other way. **Demonstrate** how it is to be made.

After you have demonstrated the stroke, have the children **practice both** the backward- and forward-slanting lines on the board. When you are sure the **children know the difference** between the two lines, have them **go to their desks** and **proceed** with the lesson.

Again, in row three be sure the children are drawing slanted lines, not almost vertical lines.

Possibly at the end of this lesson, you might like to **give a short quiz** to your children to **test their comprehension of the different lines.** Send the children to the board (on paper would be all right too), call out the names of the lines in varying order, and have them draw the line that you have specified. (This suggestion could also be used as a separate lesson in itself.)

Lesson 6
Lines That Go Around (Circles)

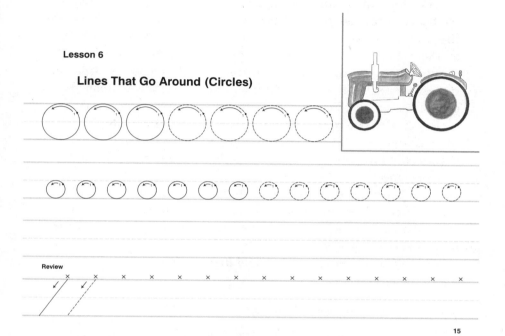

Aim of the Lesson

To teach the circle stroke.

Directions

In rows one and two, have the children draw over each solid and dotted circle several times *continuously*. They should begin at each dot and follow the arrow. In row three, the children should fill the row half with large circles and half with small circles. Row four is a review of the forward-slanting line. Have the children draw forward-slanting lines, beginning each one at the *x*.

Conducting the Class

Ask the children:

"How many of you know what we call the kind of lines that you see on this page?" (Circles.)

"What does the tractor have that looks like circles?" (Tires.)

The children should watch you closely as you **draw a circle** on the board. Then ask them if they can tell **the difference between the circle and the lines** they drew in previous lessons. Help them to understand that a **circle is a line that bends around until it touches itself again at the beginning point.** It looks like **one continuous line.** Unlike a straight line, when the circle is finished, you cannot easily tell where it began and where it ended.

Emphasize **the place of beginning for the circle stroke.** If the circle is begun on **the upper right side** of the circle (especially rather than at the top), there will not as likely be a sharp point where the two ends meet.

Send the children to the board to **draw over circles that you have placed there for them** (you may want to use a chalk compass). They should trace around the circles a number of times to **get the feel of the circle stroke.**

At their seats, the children should **proceed** with the lesson according to the directions above.

Further Helps for the Teacher

It will be the **rare child** that will be able to draw a **perfectly round circle the first time.** But you should work with the children until you are satisfied that they are drawing them as nearly round as they are able. The more they practice, the more their circles will improve.

Plenty of practice is in order for this lesson. The circle stroke is one of the most important strokes, for **much of the success of the child** in handwriting **depends upon him being able to make curved lines smoothly and accurately.** Work hard on both the smoothness and accurateness of the circle. **Smoothness involves not making a lot of jerky strokes with small points here and there on the circle.** An accurate circle is one that is round rather than oval or some other odd shape. Most of your problems in teaching the circle stroke will fall into these two areas.

Lesson 7
Lines That Curve (Part Circles)

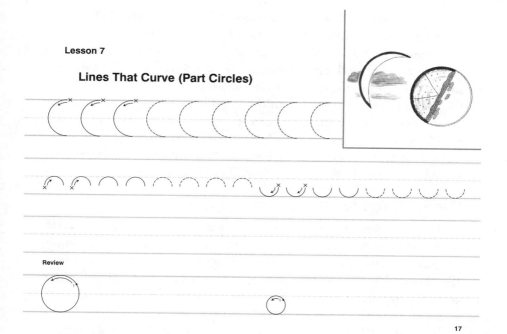

Aim of the Lesson

To teach the curve, or part-circle, stroke.

Directions

The children should trace and retrace over the solid and dotted lines in rows one and two, following the direction of the arrows. In row three, four of each kind of curve should be drawn (twelve altogether). Row four is a review of the circle. The children should trace over the two circles already there and then fill the first space with large circles and the second space with small circles.

Conducting the Class

Open the class period by **discussing the relationship between** the **curve stroke** and **the two items in the picture** at the top of the page. The children should compare the moon as shown with a full moon, a half pie with a whole pie, and then a part circle with a full circle.

Using the board for demonstration, **explain the difference between a curve and a full circle.** Explain that the curve does not go far enough around to meet itself at the starting point, although it curves just as does the circle stroke. **Draw a full circle** on the board **along with a curve,** for their comparison.

Explain carefully to the children just **where they are to begin each stroke.** They should **retrace each stroke several times**. Check again (as you should each class period) to be sure the children have good posture, are holding their pencils correctly, and have their lesson pages positioned correctly on their desk tops.

Further Helps for the Teacher

In this lesson we are **not** showing curve strokes **in every position and size** in which they are found in the alphabet. In teaching the alphabet, we will come across curve strokes that are different from the three shown here. **The goal** of this lesson is to **help the child to differentiate between the part- and full-circle strokes** and to **learn to make a simple curve line.**

You will again want to **stress making a smooth curve,** without jerky moves. In some children **jerkiness** will be **a result of tenseness and nervousness,** while in others it will be **because they are writing too slowly.** You will need to judge which is true in each case and then work with it accordingly.

If you would like to give your children extra practice, have them copy each stroke in the space directly above or below it.

Lesson 8
Preview of Manuscript Strokes

Lesson 8

Review of Manuscript Strokes

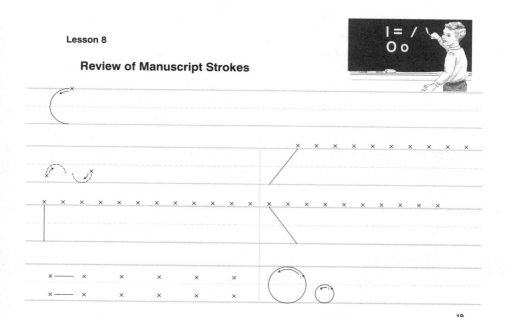

19

Aim of the Lesson

To review the basic manuscript strokes.

Directions

In each row have the children first trace over the strokes that are already there. The children should fill out the spaces allotted following each stroke, working down the left side first and then down the right.

Conducting the Class

Test your children on their memory by **asking them if they can remember** without looking **the picture that went with each**

39

lesson. First give them the name of the line and have them tell you the picture that matches; then you give the picture and have them tell you the name of the line that matches. So that you do not have to look back for this, here they are:

down line—telephone poles
across line—steps on a ladder
backward-slanting line—boy hoeing
forward-slanting line—girl on a sliding board
circle—tractor tires
curve—moon and a half pie

This will help them to establish the identity of each line.

Explain to the children that **they have now learned all the lines they need to make the letters of the alphabet.** So it is very **important that they remember the names of the different lines** and **how to make them.** Explain that **in the lesson today they will draw each line over again** several times to help them remember it. Look over the lesson with the children, and **be sure they can identify each line.**

The curve (part-circle) stroke is reviewed first and more extensively because this is the only review for it in this section.

Further Helps for the Teacher

Your children should have reached these goals by this time:

1. They should **understand correct posture** and **correct pencil holding.**
2. They should know **how to hold a piece of chalk correctly.**
3. They should be able to **make each manuscript stroke fairly smoothly and accurately,** and be able to **associate it with its name.**
4. They should understand that the lines they have learned to make are the lines that make up all the letters of the alphabet.

During this lesson, you should be sure that each child is achieving these goals. If any is not, now is the time to work with him. Remember that **if the child does not yet know his strokes, he is really not ready to begin learning his letters.**

Keep in mind also that the letters formed with either forward- or backward-slanting strokes require **varying degrees of slant** in order to be made correctly.

Lesson 9
Test of Manuscript Strokes

Lesson 9

Test of Manuscript Strokes

21

Aim of the Lesson

To test the children's understanding of the basic manuscript strokes.

Directions for Giving the Test

Before giving the test, **make sure the children are sitting straight and holding their pencils correctly.**

As you **give the names of the strokes,** the children should **make at least three of each one.** They should start a new row each time they write a new stroke, going **down the left side first** and then **down the right side.**

Test

1. large circle
2. backward-slanting line
3. down line
4. small circle
5. large curve
6. small curve (upper or lower)
7. forward-slanting line
8. across line

Further Helps for the Teacher

As a teacher, you should look over this test before giving it to your children, to be sure that it matches their general understanding. Do not be afraid to make changes or rearrangements according to your understanding of your children's learning and ability up to this point, as long as you are confident that they have achieved the goals outlined in Lesson 8.

In evaluating this test, grade on the basis of what the class as a whole understands and whether each child is working up to the limits of his ability. **Do not allow any child to do less than his best.**

Unit 2

Forming
Small Letters

Lessons 10–51

Lesson 10
The Letter l

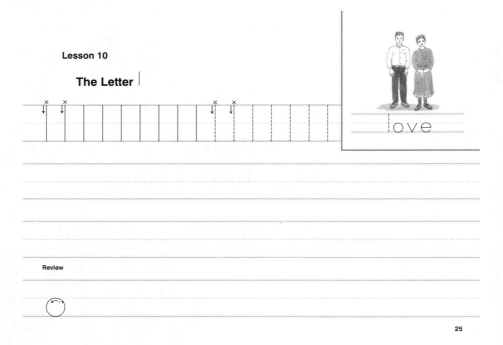

Aim of the Lesson

To introduce the alphabet, make the letter *l*, and help the children learn to write their first names.

Directions

Have the children trace over the solid and dotted letters in row one. In row two they should practice the letter *l* on their own. Row three is for name-writing practice. Row four is a review of the small circle. The children should fill out the row with small circles.

Conducting the Class

Have the children open their books to the alphabet inside the book cover. The first thing to do in this class period is to **introduce them to the small letter alphabet.** They may have already been introduced to the alphabet in the area of letter recognition, but you must help them to look at the letters from the writing angle. As they look over the letters with you, remind them that all these letters are made up of the lines they have been learning. Give them the opportunity to try to find in the letters the different lines they have already learned.

Now turn back to Lesson 10. Before talking about the letter *l*, **look with the children at the picture and word in the corner of the page.** The children should **trace over the dotted letter** after looking at the lesson title. Explain to the children that they should be thankful that God loves them enough to give them parents who love and care for them.

Proceeding with the lesson, **demonstrate the letter *l*** on the blackboard. Explain that the letter *l* is made exactly like one of the lines they have already learned. Try to get them to tell you which one it is (down line). **After blackboard practice** (if feasible), **have them go ahead with rows one, two, and four.**

After these rows are completed, you should **help your children learn to write their names.** Some may already know how but may be spelling incorrectly, writing letters backward, and suchlike. Those who do not know how to write their names should learn by copying the letters from the alphabet. **They should use row three for practice with this.** Give them individual help as needed. Until they learn the letters, be satisfied if they can write their names well enough that you can identify them. As they learn the letters in the lessons to follow, check up on their name writing to be sure they are putting to practice what they have learned.

Now is a good time to check on the starting and stopping points of your children's down lines. They should not be running over the lines either above or below.

Lesson 11
The Letter i

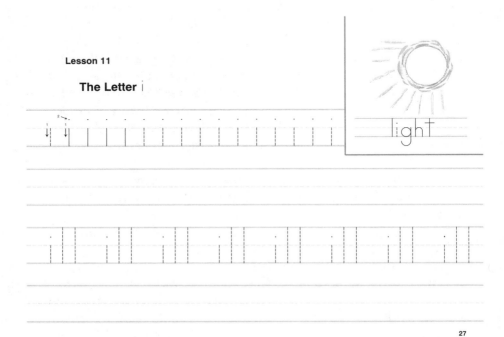

Lesson 11

The Letter i

light

27

Aim of the Lesson

To teach the manuscript letter i.

Directions

The children should trace over the solid and dotted letters in row one. Row two is for practice. In row three, the word *ill* is to be traced over each time. Row four is a review of the manuscript strokes. The children are to make the different strokes as you call them out (see "Conducting the Class").

Conducting the Class

Look at the picture at the top of the page. Explain that God made the sun, which gives light. But God is even brighter than the sun. God is so bright that ordinary people cannot look on Him at all. When we get to heaven, we will need different eyes so that we can look at God. Have the children **trace over the dotted letter** *i* in the word *light*.

Turn back to the alphabet before explaining the letter. **Have the children look over the alphabet and find the letter** *i* **there.**

Compare the letter *i* **and the letter** *l* of the previous lesson. The letter *i* is similar to the letter *l* in that it is a down line. It is different in that it starts from the middle rather than from the top and it has a dot above the top of the line.

Explain to the children that **the letter** *i* **is a two-step letter.** The first step is to draw a down line from the middle to the bottom, and the second step is to place a dot directly above the line.

After you have demonstrated, explained the letter, and given some blackboard practice, **have the children proceed with the lesson.**

For the review line, call out these strokes for the children to make:

down line	backward-slanting line
small curve (upper or lower)	small circle
forward-slanting line	across line

Further Helps for the Teacher

Row three, as in this lesson, will be a feature of some lessons. In this row we are putting letters that the children have already learned together to form simple words. It is to serve two purposes: more review, and preparation for word writing later on. You may need to explain some words to the children if they do not understand them.

Be sure the children are putting their dots where they belong. They should be not only directly above the line but also the right distance above. The dots should be placed a little less than halfway between the top and middle lines. Be sure the children always draw the line first before placing the dot.

By this time the children should have had enough practice with drawing down lines that they should be able to make them fairly straight and accurate. You should be working hard with any students who have problems in this area.

Lesson 12

The Letter t

Lesson 12

The Letter †

Truth

29

Aim of the Lesson

To teach the manuscript letter *t*.

Directions

The children are to trace over the solid and dotted letters in row one. Row two is for their practice of the letter *t*. In row three they are to trace over the letters of the word *lit*. Row four is a review of the letter *i*. They should trace the one letter that is already there and fill the remainder of the row with *i*'s of their own.

48

Conducting the Class

After looking at the *t*'s in the lesson, **have the children trace over the dotted *t* in the word** *truth* **in the picture** at the top of the page. Some of the children may know the word. See if they can tell you why there is a picture of the Bible along with the word *truth*. **Explain** that everything God says in the Bible is *true*; that is why it is the truth. To be like God, we need to tell the truth also.

Let the children find the letter *t* in the alphabet. They should be able to **identify the two strokes** in this letter (down and across). Remind the children of the formation of the letters *i* and *l*; **then compare the letter *t* strokewise, with those two letters.

In **explaining** the **formation** of the letter *t*, **demonstrate on the blackboard.** Show that *t* **is also a two-step letter** by drawing the down line as the first step and then the across line as the second step. Show the children just where the across line is to be placed in relation to the middle line and the top line a little less than halfway up from the middle line).

Explain the word *lit* as it is used in these sentences: He lit the fire, or, We lit a candle.

When you have finished your explanation, you may **give the children some blackboard practice** and **have them proceed with the lesson.** Supervise their work carefully.

Further Helps for the Teacher

There are several ways to print the letter *t*. **We have chosen to make it full height with the "cross" above the center line.** It also **lacks a curve** at the bottom as used by some systems. In our minds, this style seems to be more simple and efficient.

One thing you will need to watch for as the children cross their *t*'s is **the height of the "cross" on the stem.** The children may have a tendency to make it either too near the middle line or too near the top.

Also some students may get the **"cross" slanted.** Remind them that the "cross" is an *across* line, not a backward- or forward-slanting line. It should be perpendicular to the stem.

You will also need to watch that the **"crosses" do not become lopsided.** There should be the same length of line on each side of the down line. You may wish to illustrate various errors that should be avoided.

Lesson 13
The Numerals 1 and 4

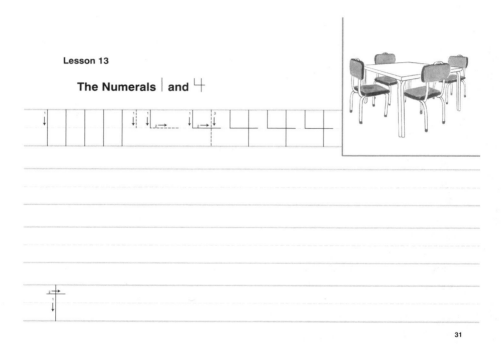

Aim of the Lesson

To teach the proper formation of the numerals *1* and *4*.

Directions

In row one, the children should trace over each numeral. In rows two and three, they should practice each numeral in the spaces directly below the already existing numerals. Row four is a review of the letter *t*. After tracing the letter, the children should fill out the rest of the row with *t*'s of their own.

Conducting the Class

To open the class discussion, call the children's attention to the picture in the corner of the page. Ask them first to count the number of tables in the picture and then the number of chairs. Tell them that the numbers they gave are the numbers they will learn to write in today's lesson. They will be learning to write numbers along with the letters. Just as they will need letters for writing words, so they will need numbers for counting and figuring.

Looking at **the numeral 1**, the children will be quick to see that this number **is identical to the letter** *l* and is composed of just one down line. While they are no doubt familiar with the numeral *1*, you will want to **have them practice it a few times to get the form established in their minds.**

The numeral *4* will take a little more explanation. Explain that it is not a two-step but **a three-step figure.** It is made up of three separate strokes. **The first two strokes are made without lifting the pencil.** First a down line is drawn from the top line to the middle line; then an across line is drawn along the middle line. The across line should be somewhat longer than the down line (about 1 1/2 times as long). The third stroke, also a down line, begins at the top line and goes all the way to the bottom. It should be aimed so as to cross the across line at a place that will leave a little line to the right of the crossing point.

Have the children practice the numeral *4* **extensively on the blackboard** before they begin working on their lesson. This will help you to help them more effectively.

Further Helps for the Teacher

Your greatest difficulties in teaching the numeral *4* will likely be in relation to the crossing of the second and third strokes. The children may have a **tendency to place the third stroke too far to the left or the right.** If this is learned incorrectly now, it may become a permanent habit.

Some children may also have trouble **making the second stroke as long as it should be.** This will definitely affect the appearance of the numeral and cause problems with the third stroke. The enclosed part of the numeral should, when finished, form **three sides of a square.**

Lesson 14
Review of Stick Letters

Lesson 14

Review of Stick Letters

33

Aim of the Lesson

To review the letters *l, i, t,* and the numerals *1* and *4.*

Directions

Each letter or numeral should be traced over and then copied in the spaces following each one, until the spaces are filled.

Conducting the Class

Explain to the children that this lesson is a **review of the five letters and numerals** they have learned to write. These five are called **stick letters.** Stick letters look a little like their name suggests—sticks. They are made up basically of down lines and across lines.

For review, give the children an oral drill. Let them tell you the letters and numerals they have learned so far and the strokes (in proper order) that make up each letter and numeral. It would be good to mix them up as you give them out. Review as much as necessary until you are sure they have a grasp of these letters and numerals. Following are the ones learned thus far with the strokes that compose them:

l—down line
i—down line, dot
t—down line, across line
1—down line
4—down line, across line, down line.

Have the children proceed with the lesson.

Further Helps for the Teacher

These are some goals that you should have achieved by this time:

1. The children should be able to understand and put into practice the **principles of letter formation for the five letters and numerals** learned thus far.
2. Correct **posture and pencil holding** should be becoming more automatic. (You should not need to remind them so frequently.)
3. They should be **acquainted with the alphabet** well enough that they can find the letters they need beyond those they have learned to write.
4. They should be able to **write** at least **their first name.**

A review lesson can be very valuable to the teacher for evaluation. Take this opportunity to check over your children's papers and compare them with each other and with your goals for their work. **Be sure you are setting your goals high enough** so that the children learn to make their letters accurately, right from the beginning.

Lesson 15
The Letter o

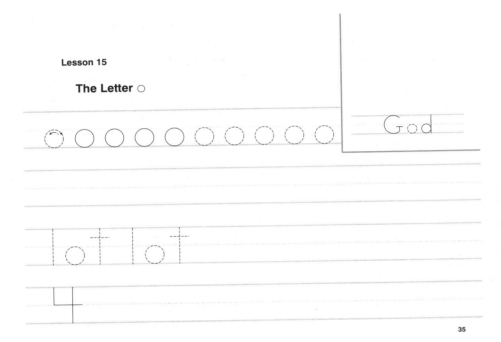

Lesson 15

The Letter ○

God

lot lot

4

35

Aim of the Lesson

To teach the manuscript letter *o*.

Directions

The children should trace over the solid and dotted letters in row one. Row two is for practice of the letter *o*. The word *lot*, in row three, is to be traced over each time. The last part of the row is for practice of the letter *o*. Row four is a review of the numeral *4*. The numeral is to be traced over and copied in the remainder of the space.

Conducting the Class

Look with the children at the word *God* at the top of the page. Ask the children if they can tell **why there is no picture with the word** *God*. (We cannot see God.) We know much about God from the Bible, but no one has ever seen the face of God Himself. Even though we have never seen Him, we know that He is, because the Bible tells us so.

Explain to the children that with this lesson they will begin learning to **form letters** that are **made with circles.** We will begin with the **simplest of them, the letter** *o*.

The children should **find the letter** *o* **in the alphabet.** They should quickly recognize this letter, because it is made the same as the circle stroke. Explain that this letter should not be too difficult to make, because they have actually been making it already.

The letter *o* is a **one-step letter.** It is composed of one small circle drawn neatly and correctly.

After **you have demonstrated** the letter, **have the children practice it** on the blackboard and then proceed with the lesson according to the directions.

Further Helps for the Teacher

The suggestions given for the teaching of the circle stroke (Lesson 6) apply also to the letter *o*. Throughout this portion on circle letters, you will be working on some problems that are peculiar to the formation of circles.

One important thing to strive for in helping the children with their circles is **smoothness.** Encourage them to make the complete circle without stopping here and there to see how their circle is coming along. This is one of the **chief causes of jerky formation of circles.**

After they have made some progress in smoothness, help them also to make their circles accurately. To accomplish this, they should have some circle-making practice on the blackboard or on paper each day while learning full-circle letters.

Lesson 16
The Numeral 0

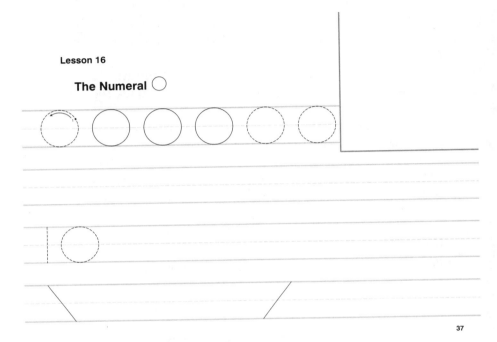

The Numeral ○

37

Aim of the Lesson

To teach the numeral *0*.

Directions

The children should trace over the solid and dotted *0*'s in row one. In row two they should practice the numeral *0*. The *10* in row three should be traced over and copied to the end of the row. Row four is a review of the backward-slanting and forward-slanting lines. The children should copy each stroke several times in the spaces following.

56

Conducting the Class

Ask the children:

"What do you see in the 'picture' at the top of the page?" (Nothing.)

"What number means nothing?" (Zero [0].)

"Do you see a number on the page that needs a zero to make it mean what it does?" (Yes; *10*.)

"What would happen if you left the zero off the number *10*?" (It would become the number *1*.)

(Drawing the children's attention to the blackboard, form a *0* and an *o*.) "How does the numeral *0* look like the letter *o* learned in yesterday's lesson?" (They are both circles.)

"How are they different?" (Zero [0] is one *large* circle, and *o* is one *small* circle.)

"How many steps does it take to make the numeral *0*?" (One.)

Send the children **to the board for practice.** Work to improve the **quality** of their circles in **smoothness and accuracy** (see Lesson 15, "Further Helps for the Teacher"). Also emphasize **the place of beginning in writing a circle.**

Have the children proceed with the lesson according to the directions.

Further Helps for the Teacher

Since your children are not learning something totally new in this lesson, now would be a good time to check on them in a few other areas.

Check on their posture. Do they maintain right habits of posture throughout the class period? Or do they begin the class with correct posture and then revert to incorrect habits later on?

Also check to see how much your children lean over when they work. They should be able to **write well when leaning forward just slightly** in their seats. Unless their eyes need attention, they should not need to bring their eyes within just a few inches of the paper.

Pay attention to your **left-handed** children. Are they developing a hooked wrist? If so, they need to be helped now, before the habit becomes established.

Lesson 17
The Letter a

Lesson 17

The Letter a

ͻ a⌄ a a a a a a a a | Thanks

Tail Tail

⌒ ⌣

39

Aim of the Lesson

To teach the manuscript letter a.

Directions

Have the children trace over the letter a in row one. In row two, the children should practice the letter. In row three the word *tail* should be traced over each time. The remainder of the row should be used for continued practice of the letter a. Row four is a review of the curve. Each stroke should be traced over and copied in the spaces following.

Conducting the Class

Ask the children:

"How often do you do what this child is doing?" (Probably three times a day.)

"Why do you do this?" (To thank God for your food.)

Briefly explain the importance of giving thanks to God at each meal. Have the children trace over the dotted *a* in the word *thanks*.

After the children have **found the letter *a* in the alphabet, demonstrate it** on the blackboard. Have the **children tell you how many steps it takes to make** this letter. Explain that **one complete circle** is to be drawn first, beginning at the proper place. After the completion of the circle, **a down line** is drawn down the right side of the circle, touching the circle.

Following **blackboard practice,** the children should **proceed with their lesson** according to the directions.

Further Helps for the Teacher

One problem that will likely arise in teaching the letter *a* is difficulty in making the *down line and the circle join correctly.* If the two are joined correctly, the circle should not extend beyond the down line to leave a space on the other side. Some children may tend to the opposite extreme and not allow their circle and down stroke to touch at all, giving the letter the appearance of two separate letters, *o* and *i.* Also, the down line should follow the circle edge for some distance, not simply touch the circle at one small point.

Some teachers may feel that it is simpler to teach the letter *a* in a **manner that avoids lifting the pencil.** It is definitely a faster method, but since **it deviates from the stroke approach,** we are not teaching it here in favor of the simple circle and down-stroke method.

You should begin to **pay** special **attention to your children's letter spacing** in the row. Usually children have **a tendency to crowd** their letters. The letters in row two should be spaced very much like the ones in row one.

Do your children have a tendency to get finished with the practice (second) row before you have an opportunity to look at their work? If so, **have them do only half the row and then stop to give you time to make corrections and suggestions.** When you have checked the work of each individual student, he may go ahead and **finish the row.**

Lesson 18

The Letter e

Lesson 18

The Letter e

e e e e e e e e

s e e d

t e l l   t e l l

a

41

Aim of the Lesson

To teach the manuscript letter *e*.

Directions

The children are to first trace over the letter *e* in row one. In row two, the letter should be practice-written. In row three, the word *tell* is to be traced over each time. The end of the row is to be used for practice of the letter *e*. Row four is a review of the letter *a*. It is to be traced over and copied to the end of the row.

Conducting the Class

Ask the children:

"What is the girl in the picture dropping into the ground?" (A seed.)

"What usually happens when a seed is planted in the ground?" (It grows up into a plant.")

"What makes it grow?" (Sunshine, air, water, God.)

Explain briefly to the children that God sends to the earth all the different things that make plants grow from seeds. Have the children trace over the two dotted *e*'s in the word *seed*.

As the children look at the letter *e*, **they should pick out the two strokes that compose it.** They should find an **across** stroke and a **curve** stroke. Explain that although this curve, or part-circle, stroke does not look exactly like the ones they drew earlier, it is still a part circle because it does not make a complete circle.

Have the children form letters along with you, on the blackboard or on paper. Explain the formation of the letter **as follows:**

"Begin with a short across line drawn halfway between the bottom and middle lines. From the end of the across line, a curve is drawn up and around, touching the beginning point of the across line and continuing until it makes almost a complete circle. When the line stops, there should be a small space left."

After they have completed row one, **have them practice the letter on writing paper** (or the back of their lesson page) under your supervision before they do the rest of the lesson.

Further Helps for the Teacher

Although the letter *e* is not a full-circle letter, it is being taught at this point because it is one of the most frequently used letters of the alphabet. It is similar enough to a full-circle letter that it can easily be taught among those letters.

The letter *e* is one of the more difficult letters to learn. To help the children with their problems in forming this letter, draw their attention continually to the strokes which compose this letter. **Show them where their stroke is incorrectly made, rather than telling them their letter is incorrectly made.** This will also help reinforce the strokes of the letter in your child's mind.

One problem some children have with this letter is **not closing**

the upper half-circle of the letter as they come around with their curve. This problem is often **a result of not making the across line long enough.** Then a well-rounded curve stroke will not easily touch the across line without bending out of proportion.

Also as the children pick up speed in making this letter, you may find a **rounded corner appearing at the junction of the two strokes,** rather than a sharp one. Impress upon them the importance of **making the two strokes distinct** from each other. In some cases it may be necessary to make the children lift their pencils each time at the end of the first stroke.

If the letter is inclined to be **too narrow or too squat,** the problem is in the formation of the circle. If this is the problem, have the child practice, first the complete circle stroke and then with gaps, as in the letter *e*.

Do not let the children **bring the tail of the letter out too straight** at the end. The tail should be aimed at the corner of the two strokes, headed toward the completion of a full circle, only stopping before it gets there.

Lesson 19
The Letter b

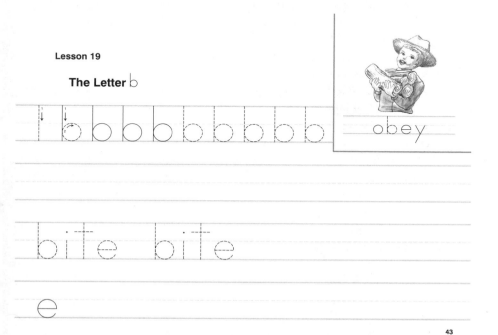

Lesson 19

The Letter b

obey

bite bite

e

43

Aim of the Lesson

To teach the manuscript letter *b*.

Directions

The children should trace over the strokes and letters in row one. In row two they should practice the letter *b*. In row three the word *bite* is to be traced over each time, with the end of the row to be used for continued practice of the letter *b*. Row four is a review of the letter *e*. It should be traced over and copied to the end of the row.

Conducting the Class

Ask these questions in relation to the picture at the top of the page:
"What does it mean to obey?" (To do what you are told.)
"This boy is carrying in wood to obey his parents; what are some things you do to obey your parents?"
"Should you obey your parents cheerfully?" (Yes.)

Following the above discussion, have the children **trace over the dotted letter** b in the word *obey*.

Have the children **find the letter** b **in the alphabet** and look at it carefully. They should see quite readily that it is **made up of two strokes,** a **down line** and a **circle.** It somewhat resembles the letter *l* stuck to the letter *o*. While demonstrating on the blackboard, **explain** the formation of the letter. A down line is drawn first, two spaces high. After the pencil is lifted, it should be placed on the down line halfway between the bottom and middle lines. From this point a small circle is drawn in the direction opposite from usual. It travels backward. Since the children are not used to making **backward circles,** you may want to **have them practice them on the board** before they practice the letter as a whole.

As the children proceed with the lesson, check again on their **posture and pencil-holding** habits.

Further Helps for the Teacher

As you should have noticed, the circle stroke for the letter *b* is being made in reverse of the normal circle stroke. The children should not have much difficulty with this due to their familiarity with the normal circle stroke.

As in the lesson on the letter *a*, be sure the **circle** and the **down line are joining correctly.** The same basic rules for the letter *a* apply to the letter *b*, except that with the letter *b* the down line is made before the circle is made. This will likely make it easier for your children to join this letter correctly.

Check to be sure the children are making their **down lines straight up and down, not slanted.** Also be sure they are drawing their **circles accurately.** Their letters should not look like these: ʙ ᖯ ᑲ ᖯ.

Some children may be inclined to make their circles to the left of the down lines, without realizing that they are **forming the letter** *d* **rather than the letter** *b*. Those who do this, generally do it only part of the time; but be sure you correct it whenever you see it.

64

Lesson 20
The Letter d

Lesson 20

The Letter d

door

dot   dot

45

Aim of the Lesson

To teach the manuscript letter *d*.

Directions

The children should trace over the strokes and letters in row one. Row two is for practice of this letter. In row three, the word *dot* is to be traced over each time. The children should use the end of the row to continue practicing the letter *d*. The letter *b*, which is reviewed in row four, should be traced over and then copied to the end of the row.

Conducting the Class

Ask the children these questions:

"What do you see in the picture?" (A door.)

"What is a door used for?" (To make a way to get into a building or room, to keep out the weather or to keep out noise.)

"What is one thing you need to remember when you open or close a door?" (Close it quietly; do not slam it.)

Following the above exercise, **have the children trace over the dotted letter** *d* **in the picture** to complete the word *door.*

The children should **find the letter** *d* **in the alphabet.** Then place the two letters *d* and *b* **on the blackboard.** Help them **compare the two letters.** Both *d* and *b* contain down lines that are two spaces tall. Both contain small circles. The difference between the two letters is that the circles are on opposite sides of the down lines. The circle is on the forward side for the letter *b* and on the backward side for the letter *d.*

Now **looking more specifically at the letter** *d*, explain to the children how it is made. The **circle stroke** is formed **first,** in the normal way. The **down line** is drawn so as to **join the circle stroke** along the right side.

After some **blackboard practice,** have the children **proceed with the lesson** according to the directions.

Further Helps for the Teacher

In order **to help your children distinguish between the letters** *d* **and** *b,* you may want to give them a **short quiz** on the blackboard. Tell them to write down each letter as they hear it. Give out the letters in such a manner that the children do not know which one is coming next. By doing this, you will strengthen the letter forms in the minds of all the children and will discover any problems your children may have in differentiating between these two letters.

The joining of strokes will again require special attention. Although *d* is made very much like *a,* the extra length at the top of the *d* makes it difficult to aim accurately from the top line to the right side of the circle. **The tendency will be to start from such a point that the line needs to slant in order to join the circle stroke correctly.** Call this to the children's attention if they have a problem with it. To overcome it will simply take practice.

Lesson 21
The Letter p

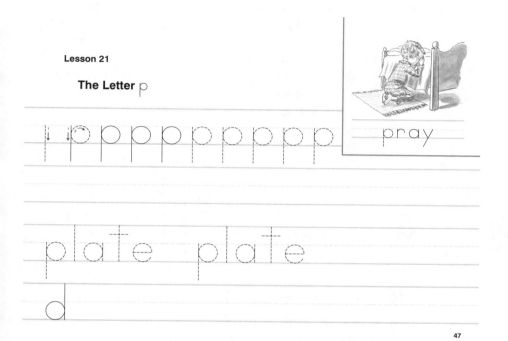

Lesson 21

The Letter p

pray

plate plate

47

Aim of the Lesson

To teach the manuscript letter *p*.

Directions

Have the children trace over the strokes of the letter *p* in row one. Row two is for practice of this letter. They should trace over the word *plate* each time in row three and then continue practice of the letter *p* in the last part. In row four, which is a review of the letter *d*, the letter is to be traced over and then copied to the end of the row.

Conducting the Class

The picture in today's lesson should remind the children of the picture in Lesson 17. Tell them that it is not only at mealtime that we pray and thank God for His gifts to us. Another good time to pray is at night before we go to sleep, as this child is doing.

Have the children **trace over the dotted letter** *p* **in the word** *pray.*

Looking now at the letter *p*, have the children again **do some comparing. The letters** *b*, *d*, **and** *p* **are all made of the same strokes,** a down line and a circle. **The main difference is in how the strokes are arranged.** The letter *p* is made exactly like the letter *b*, except that the down line is as if it had slipped down a space so that it runs from the middle line to one space below the bottom line.

To form the letter *p*, the down line is made first. It begins at the middle line and goes down the full distance of a tall down line. The next step is to draw a circle beginning at the down line between the middle and bottom lines, making a reverse circle.

Have the children **trace over the letters in the first row** before they practice on the blackboard, **so that they have a clearer perception of the proper length of the down line.** Following blackboard practice, have the children **proceed with the lesson** according to the directions.

Further Helps for the Teacher

Probably the **greatest difficulty** your children will have with this letter is in **knowing how far to extend its tail.** Until repeated practice produces greater familiarity, you could establish "almost to the top line of the next row, but not quite" as the proper length. Also you could explain that there should be about the same amount of line below the bottom line as there is between the bottom and middle lines. This would give them a good start in the idea of proportion.

Since the method of **joining strokes is the same as with the letter** *b*, you will want to watch for the same problems in joining as with that letter.

If you have time, you may want to **test your children's memory of manuscript strokes,** since it has been some time since they have learned them. Place the basic strokes on the board, and have the children name them. As an additional exercise, have them draw each stroke as you name it.

Lesson 22
The Letter g

Lesson 22

The Letter g

gift

glad get

p

49

Aim of the Lesson

To teach the manuscript letter *g*.

Directions

Have the children trace over the strokes and letters in row one. In row two the children should practice the letter *g* on their own. In row three, they should trace over the two words printed there and practice the letter *g* in the rest of the row. Row four is a review of the letter *p*. The children should trace over the letter and copy it to the end of the row.

Conducting the Class

Ask the children:

"Who gives you more gifts than anyone else?" (God.)

"What are some of the gifts He gives you?" (Friends, parents, food, and so on.)

Have the children trace over the dotted letter *g* **in the word** *gift*.

Draw the letter *g* on the blackboard. Have the children look at the letter and **pick out the first stroke they recognize in the letter.** This will likely be the circle stroke. Continue by **asking them to identify another stroke, and still another,** in the letter. They should find a down line and a curve. **Ask them if this letter reminds them of any letter** they have already learned. They might say the letter *p*. This is a valid observation because both letters have parts that go below the bottom line. The letter *g* is similar also to the letter *d*, only the down line has slipped down a space and a curve has been added at the bottom.

The letter *g* is a **three-stroke** letter but only a **two-step** letter. The first stroke is written by itself, but the **last two strokes are put together** so that you do not think of them as being two separate strokes.

As you explain, demonstrate. Have the children watch you carefully. The first stroke is a full circle. The second stroke is a down line, which begins at the middle line, touches the right side of the circle, and goes down some distance below the bottom line about three-eighths inch). It **does not go down as far as the down line of the letter** *p*, because if it did, **there would not be any room for the curve on the bottom,** which is the third stroke. The curve begins right where the down line stops. One should not lift his chalk or pencil, but curve right down, around, and back up.

Following explanation and practice, have the children **proceed** with the lesson according to the directions.

Further Helps for the Teacher

Following are some **problems** your children may have in forming this letter:

1. A **proper transition from the down line to the curve** at the bottom is necessary. Some children may omit the down line altogether below the bottom line and begin curving far

too early. This makes the g look as thought it is leaning to the side. Remind your children of this, and it may help them, to remember to begin the curve stroke farther down.

2. The **curve may also be drawn out too wide,** making an extraordinarily long tail.

3. **Sometimes the down line is made too long before the curve begins,** leaving little room for the curve to round out below. This will tend to make the curve too shallow and flat-bottomed. Tell the children who have this problem that their curves should be round enough to make the g look as if it is going to roll over at any time (though, of course, it should not actually be doing it!).

Lesson 23
The Letter q

Lesson 23

The Letter q

quiet

quail

g

51

Aim of the Lesson

To teach the manuscript letter q.

Directions

The children should trace over the strokes and letters in row one. In row two they should practice the letter *q*. In row three, the word *quail* should be traced over and then the rest of the row used to practice the letter *q*. In row four, the letter *g* is reviewed. It should be traced over and copied to the end of the row.

72

Conducting the Class

Ask the children these questions:

"Do children ever need to be quiet?" (Yes.)

"When should children be quiet?" (When they are asked or told to, in school, in church, when noise may bother others.)

Have the children **trace over the dotted letter** *q* in the word *quiet*.

Draw the two letters *g* **and** *q* on the blackboard. Try to **get the children to point out to you the difference** between the two letters. Show them that they are made very much the same but not quite.

Explain the formation of the letter *q* as follows:

"Draw a small circle between the bottom and middle lines. Next, draw a down line which begins at the middle line, touches the right side of the circle, and keeps going down until it is a little distance below the bottom line. Without lifting your pencil, draw a **curve.** It **should go in a forward direction [opposite to the letter** *g*]. At the end of the curve, stop and lift your pencil."

Following **blackboard practice and drill** (see "Further Helps for the Teacher"), have the children **proceed with the lesson** according to the directions.

Further Helps for the Teacher

Sometime soon, **you may be able to introduce the principles of drill** to your children. Place the children at the blackboard and explain that you are going to say numbers as they write the letter *q*. When you say "One," they are to draw the circle. When you say "Two," they are to make the down line. When you say "Three," they are to make the curve. Demonstrate for them several times yourself before they try to do it. **Do not go too fast** to begin with, but give them time to keep up with you. If the children become quite confused, this type of drill may be too far advanced for them at this point. Try it again later.

Be sure the children can differentiate between the letters *q* **and** *g*. Correct mistakes in this area promptly.

More space should be allowed between each *q* **than between each** *g*. Otherwise, the letters will overlap each other.

Most of the problems that were outlined for the letter *g* also apply to the letter *q*, particularly those that relate to the joining of the down line and the curve.

The letter *u* has been included in the word *quail* for the children to trace over, even though they have not yet learned the letter. The simple reasons is, of course, that to form a word, *q* must always be followed by a *u*. They will be learning the letter *u* before long, so they should go ahead and trace over it.

Lesson 24
The Numeral 9

53

Aim of the Lesson

To teach the numeral 9.

Directions

The children should trace over the strokes and numerals in row one. They should use row two for practice of the numeral 9. In row three, they should trace over the numbers printed there and then use the rest of the row for continued numeral 9 practice. Row four is a review of the letter *q*. The letter should be traced over and copied to the end of the row.

Conducting the Class

Have the children count the daisies and tulips in the picture in the corner of the page. They should find eight daisies and nine tulips. The children should tell you whether there are nine daisies or nine tulips.

The numeral 9 **is yet another figure made up of a circle and a down line. Explain** this to the children. Ask them if they can tell you of some letters that are made up of a circle and a down line. They have learned **four so far. They are** a, b, d, **and** p. The letters g and q would also fit this description, except for the curve at the bottom.

Ask the children to help you make this numeral as you proceed to place it on the blackboard. Here are some things you can ask them:

"What shall I make first, the circle or the down line?"

"Is the circle a small one or a large one?" (Draw the circle.)

"Is the down line short or tall?"

"How is the circle different from the circles in the circle letters?" (It has a "corner" on one side.)

"Now you come to the blackboard and made some 9's of your own."

Following the above demonstration and practice, proceed with the lesson according to the directions.

Further Helps for the Teacher

The numeral 9 presents a slight exception to the perfect-circle approach used in teaching the other circle letters and numerals. However, the deviation is not so great that your children should have any great difficulty in adapting to its form. You will not likely encounter many problems in teaching the numeral 9 that you have not already encountered with letters such as a and d, because their formation is very similar.

Lesson 25
The Numeral 6

Aim of the Lesson

To teach the numeral 6.

Directions

The children should trace over the strokes and numerals in row one. They should practice the numeral *6* in row two. In row three the number and word there should be traced over and the remainder of the row used for continued practice of the numeral *6*. Row four is a review of the numeral *9*. It should be traced over and copied to the end of the row.

Conducting the Class

Ask the children these questions about the picture:

"The picture shows a child about six years old. How many of you are now six years old?"

"What is one thing this child is doing that all six-year-olds should do?" (Smiling and being happy.)

"Do you think a child six years old can always be as cheerful and happy as this child is?" (Yes.)

"Since so many of you are six years old, you should enjoy learning to make the numeral 6. [Looking at the numeral.] **The numeral 6 uses** a stroke we used recently in the letters *g* and *q*, but it is used differently in this numeral. What stroke is it?" (The curve.)

"What other stroke do you see in this numeral?" (**Circle.**)

Place the numeral on the blackboard, explaining its formation as follows:

"The numeral begins with a curve. It begins at the top line. When it has reached a little below the middle line, it stops. But do not lift your pencil. Begin curving more to make a circle. The circle touches the bottom and middle lines; then it comes back to the place where it began, and stops."

Following blackboard practice, have the children **proceed** with the lesson according to the directions.

Further Helps for the Teacher

A curve line used in the numeral 6 is much more shallow than that used in the other numerals and letters. Its slanting position is also different. But it is still part of a circle, as you can demonstrate on the blackboard by drawing an oversize circle and erasing part of it. Show the children that the lower part of it is a distinct circle.

Check on your children's arm and finger movement as they write, now that they do not need to give quite as much attention to the basic strokes as at the beginning. No child should use an exclusive finger movement in making his letters. There should be some arm movement *and* some finger movement. Exclusive arm movement makes it difficult for the children to control their movements.

Lesson 26
Review of Circle Letters and Numerals

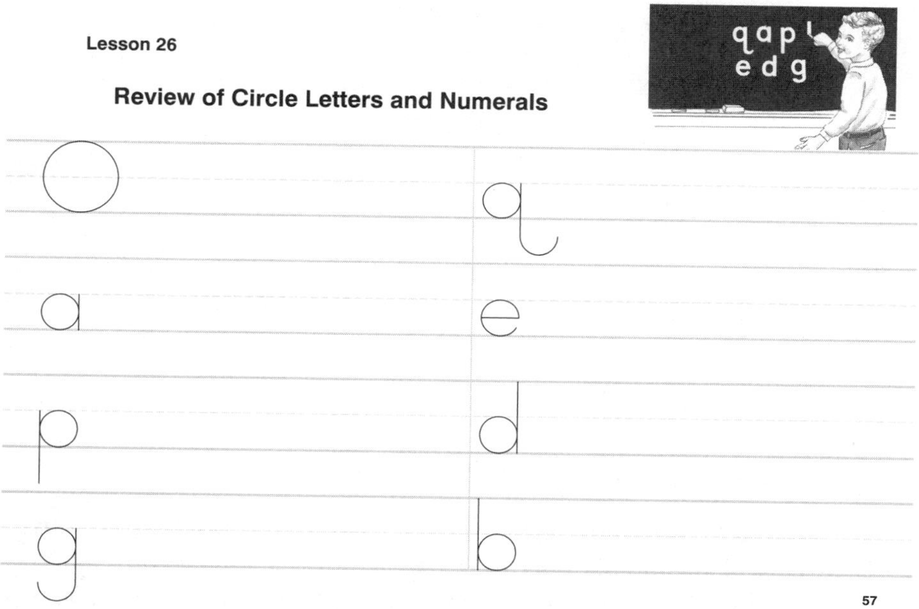

Lesson 26

Review of Circle Letters and Numerals

O

q

a

e

p

d

g

b

57

Aim of the Lesson

To thoroughly review the letters *q, a, e, p, d, g, b,* and *o* and the numerals *0, 9,* and *6.* Also the stick letters and the manuscript strokes are to be reviewed.

Directions

In each row, with the exception of the last one, the children are to trace over each letter and copy it until the row is filled. In the last row the teacher is to call all the manuscript strokes, and the children are to draw them as they are given.

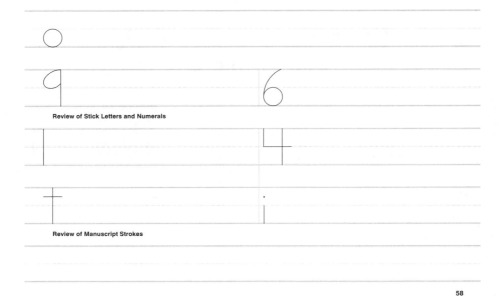

Review of Stick Letters and Numerals

Review of Manuscript Strokes

Conducting the Class

Explain to the children that **this is a review of the last eleven letters and numerals** they have learned to write, which are made with circles. They are called **circle letters, but most of these letters have other kinds of lines too.** Three have curve lines, one has an across line, and many have down lines.

The children should be given an oral drill at this point on the stroke combination of each letter and numeral that they have learned so far. Call out each child's name with a letter. Have him tell you the strokes of the letter and the order in which the strokes are made (the children may need to look at their review page to keep from getting mixed up). Or for some variation, you could have each child go to the blackboard when it is his turn and draw his letter there. He should call each stroke by name as he makes the letter (as the children have seen you do many times).

For your quick reference, **here are the circle letters with the strokes that compose them:**

o—small circle

a—circle, down line

b—down line, circle

p—down line, circle

q—circle, down line, curve

6—curve, circle.

0—large circle

e—across line, curve

d—circle, down line

g—circle, down line, curve

9—circle, down line

Further Helps for the Teacher

In addition to the goals described in Lessons 8 and 14 (look back and be sure that your children are still meeting them), **your children should have achieved the following goals in the last eleven lessons:**

1. They should **be able to understand and put into practice the principles of letter formation for the eleven letters and numerals** they have just finished learning. This includes—
   a. **greater perfection in making the circle (in smoothness and accuracy);**
   b. **learning how to join the circle to other strokes** well.
2. The children should be able to **differentiate each letter** from the others as they write them.

A review lesson is a fairer test of your children's abilities than is a regular learning lesson. **Make this lesson count more than other lessons in evaluation.** Check each paper for proper letter form and neatness. Measure each against the goals outlined above. Also include in your evaluation the children's posture and pencil-holding habits.

Lesson 27
The Letter k

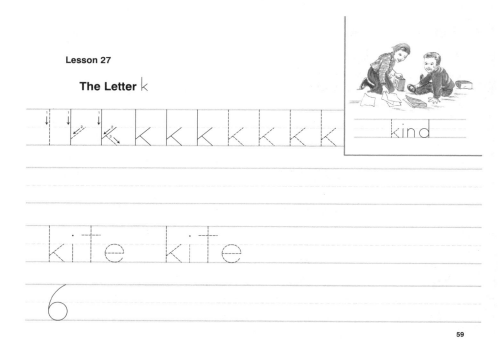

Aim of the Lesson

To teach the manuscript letter *k*.

Directions

The children are to trace over the strokes of the step-by-step illustrations and the letter *k* in row one. Row two is for more practice on the letter *k*. In row three the word *kite* is to be traced over each time. The extra space should be used to practice *k*. Row four is a review of the numeral *6*. It should be traced over and then copied in the remaining space to the end of the row.

Conducting the Class

Look with the children at the word *kind* **and at the picture** in the corner of the page. Help them to understand the meaning of kindness. The girl in the picture is showing kindness by helping one of her schoolmates after he has fallen. Children can be kind by helping their parents, grandparents, schoolmates, and anyone else they can.

The children should **trace over the dotted letter** *k* **in the word** *kind*.

With this lesson the **teaching of letters with slant strokes is begun.** To refresh the children's memory, they should **practice the backward-slanting and forward-slanting strokes** on the blackboard or on paper.

The letter *k* **is a three-step letter. Guide** the children's **attention to the first three figures** in the first row, which is a step-by-step analysis of the letter *k*. **Explain each step to them,** identifying each stroke and showing where it begins.

The following explanation is to aid your understanding of the letter. You may want to simplify it somewhat to give it to your children.

The **first stroke is a down line** from the top to the bottom. The **second stroke is a forward-slanting line** that begins at the middle line and slants down to touch the first stroke at a point about a third of the way between the middle and bottom lines (you may want to say "a little less than half"). The **third stroke is a backward-slanting line** that begins from the second stroke at a point about a third of the way between the first stroke and the middle line. It slants down to the bottom line.

Following explanation and practice, the children may proceed with the lesson.

Further Helps for the Teacher

One problem that sometimes shows up in this letter is a **tendency to bring the second and third strokes together at the same point,** like a sideways *v*. Watch for and correct this when it appears.

Both slanted lines should make about forty-five-degree angles with the first stroke. If both slants are correctly drawn, **one should be able to draw a straight line down the right side of the letter** and very nearly touch the ends of both slants. If either line is slanted too much the wrong way, it will make the right side uneven.

The third stroke should be perpendicular to the second stroke, giving the last two strokes the appearance of a lopsided capital *T*.

Some first graders tend to get this type of letter too close together. Watch for this in row two. Their letters should be about three-eighths inch apart.

Lesson 28
The Letter v

Lesson 28

The Letter ∨

voice

give give

k

61

Aim of the Lesson

To teach the manuscript letter *v*.

Directions

The children should trace over the strokes and letters in row one. In row two have them fill up the line with the letter. The word *give* in row three is to be traced over each time. The extra space is for practice of the letter *v*. Row four is a review of the letter *k*. It should be traced over and copied to the end of the row.

Conducting the Class

Ask these questions about the picture:

"What are some things you can do with your voice?" (Sing, read, speak—kindly or unkindly.)

"What are these children doing with their voices?" (Singing.)

"Is it good to sing with your voice?" (Yes; God wants us to praise Him by singing to Him and about Him.)

Have the children **trace over the dotted letter** *v* **in the word** *voice.*

As the children look at the letter v, ask them to tell you **what two kinds of lines make up this letter. Demonstrate** the letter on the board. As you do so, **give an explanation** to the children as follows:

"Begin by placing your **pencil at the middle line** where you want the letter to begin. From here **draw a backward-slanting line** to the bottom line. Do not lift your pencil but, beginning from that point, **make a forward-slanting line** up to the middle line. When you reach the middle line, stop. The letter is finished."

Send the children to the backboard and have them **first practice the forward-slanting line** going from the bottom to the top, since this is opposite from usual. Then have them practice the letter *v* itself.

Following the above explanation and practice, have the children **proceed** with the lesson according to the directions.

Further Helps for the Teacher

This letter is simple enough to make that your children should not have too much problem with it. However, there are several things that could cause some difficulty.

Watch the spread of the letter at the top. While you do not want to be too particular, if there is too much distance between the points, or too little, you should correct it.

It may also be difficult for your children to **give each line the same slant.** If this is a problem, have them practice more, concentrating on giving both lines basically the same amount of slant.

Lesson 29
The Letter w

Lesson 29

The Letter w

water

bow low

v

63

Aim of the Lesson

To teach the manuscript letter *w*.

Directions

The children should trace over the strokes and then the letters in row one. In row two they should practice the letter *w* for the length of the line. In row three, they should trace over the words *bow* and *low*. The extra space should be used to practice the letter *w*. Row four is a review of the letter *v*. The letter should be traced over and copied to the end of the row.

Conducting the Class

Ask these questions in relation to the picture:

"What do you see in the picture?" (A lake or pond.)

"What is a lake made of?" (Water.)

"Where can we get water besides from a lake?" (Rain, creeks, rivers, the ocean, the faucet.)

"What do we use water for?" (Drinking, washing, watering our garden plants.)

Tell the children we should be thankful for water. God has given it to us as a gift to use. Have them **trace over the dotted letter** *w* **in the blank space** in the word *water*.

Place the letter *w* **on the blackboard.** Looking at the general appearance of the letter, show the children that **the letter looks like two** *v*'s **placed side by side.** Although its name sounds like "double *u*," it could actually be called "double *v*," since that is how it is made.

Use the following information to help you explain the formation of the letter: The letter *w* is **composed of four strokes,** which are made without lifting the pencil. **All** the strokes **are made between the middle and bottom lines.** The **first stroke is a backward-slanting line,** which begins from the middle line and goes to the bottom line. The **second stroke is a forward-slanting line** from the bottom line back up to the middle line. **The third and fourth strokes are repeats of the first and second.**

Following your explanation, the **children should practice the letter on the blackboard.** They should make their **first letter step by step.** Discuss each stroke with them as it is made. After they have made a number of letters, send them to their seats and have them **proceed with the lesson** according to the directions.

Further Helps for the Teacher

Again, as in teaching the letter *v*, you will need to be sure that **the spread of the letter** is correct and that each **slant** is made at the same angle as each of the other slants.

Do not let the children go too fast while making this letter. The simplicity of strokes in the letter may lend itself to speed, but **accuracy demands carefulness.** If the strokes are made too rapidly, it will be difficult to be accurate in alignment. Each stroke should come right to the line, but not above or below it. Also **a very rapid**

stroke will eventually tend to produce a rounded letter on the bottom. Watch for this as the children become more experienced in making the letter.

Lesson 30
The Letter x

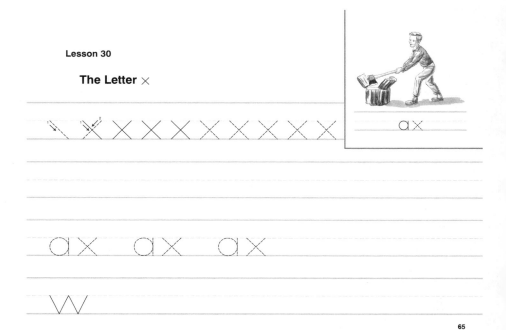

Lesson 30

The Letter ×

65

Aim of the Lesson

To teach the manuscript letter *x*.

Directions

The children should trace over the strokes and letters in row one. They should practice the letter *x* in row two. In row three they should trace over the word *ax* each time it is given and use the rest of the space for *x* practice. Row four is a review of the letter *w*. They should trace over the letter and copy it to the end of the row.

Conducting the Class

Ask these questions in relation to the picture:

"What is the man using to chop wood?" (An ax.)

"Do you have an ax at home?"

"What is an ax used for at your house?"

Have the children **trace over the dotted letter** x in the word ax.

Explain to the children that the letter x is not used very often but that we need to learn to make it anyway. There are some words, like ax, in which this letter is used.

Have the children look at the letter and **try to figure out how it is made.** They may think of several different ways to make the letter. Demonstrate on the blackboard that **the letter is really made from a backward-slanting line and a forward-slanting line.** Since this is a short letter, both lines will stay between the middle and bottom lines.

The **first stroke is the backward-slanting line.** It should slant neither too much nor too little (about a forty-five-degree angle—show correct slant as you demonstrate). **The second stroke is a forward-slanting line.** It **begins straight above the end** of the backward-slanting line. It crosses the backward-slanting line **right in the middle** and **touches the bottom line straight below the beginning** of the backward-slanting line.

Following demonstration, explanation, and **blackboard practice,** have the children **proceed with the lesson** according to the directions.

Further Helps for the Teacher

With this letter also it is important to **be sure the two lines have equal slant.** The children must begin the second stroke directly above the end of the first stroke and aim it toward a point directly below the beginning of the first stroke. If the slant of the two strokes is not equal, one line will be longer than the other, the second stroke will not cross the first stroke in the middle, and the letter will have a poor appearance.

The **slant of the strokes must be correct** as well as equal. This depends primarily on the first stroke; for if the instructions for drawing the second stroke are followed, it will always be the same angle as the first stroke. If the strokes are made too nearly horizontal, the letter will be too wide. If they are made too nearly vertical, the letter will be too narrow.

Again, you will need to watch that the children do not go so fast in making the letter that their strokes are not properly aligned at the top and bottom. **Each stroke must stop promptly at the line.**

Lesson 31
The Letter y

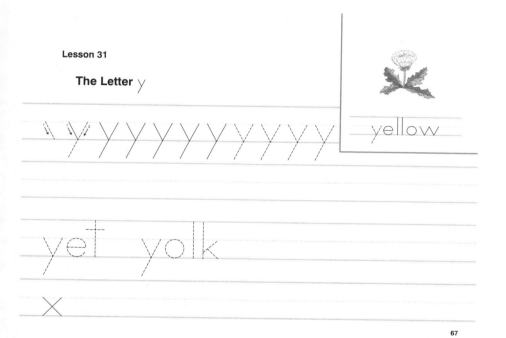

Lesson 31

The Letter y

yellow

yet   yolk

x

67

Aim of the Lesson

To teach the manuscript letter *y*.

Directions

The children should trace over the strokes and letters in row one. Row two is for practice of the letter. In row three they should trace over the words *yet* and *yolk* and then use the rest of the row to practice *y*. Row four is a review of the letter *x*. The children should trace over and copy the letter to the end of the row.

Conducting the Class

Ask the children these questions about the picture:

"What kind of flower is in the picture?" (A dandelion.)

"What color is a dandelion?" (Yellow.)

"What other things can you think of that are yellow?"

Explain that yellow is a beautiful color. God has made things in nature many beautiful colors for us to enjoy as we look at them.

Have the children **trace over the dotted letter** *y* in the word *yellow.*

Draw the letters *x* **and** *y* **on the blackboard,** and **compare the two letters.** "How is the letter *y* like the letter *x*?" (It has **two strokes,** a backward-slanting line and a forward-slanting line.) "How is it different from the letter *x*?" (In the letter *y*, the forward-slanting line goes below the bottom line, the lines do not cross in the middle, and the forward-slanting line is longer than the backward-slanting line.)

In making the letter *y*, **the backward-slanting line is drawn first.** It is made in the same way as the backward-slanting line in the letter *x* except that it does not slant quite as much. **The forward-slanting line begins at the middle line** and slants back so that it touches the end of the backward-slanting line at the bottom line. It does not stop at the bottom line but continues until it is **one space below** the bottom line. Now the letter is finished.

Following the above demonstration and explanation, give the children some **blackboard practice** and have them **proceed** with the lesson.

Further Helps for the Teacher

Watch the equality and accuracy of the slanting lines. Do not let the children slant their lines too much. Since they have just been learning the letter *x*, they may tend to do this. Remind the children that **the top of the letter** *y* **should look like the letter** *v*. If any of the children have difficulty learning the formation of *y*, tell them to begin making the letter *v* but to begin the second stroke at the top of the letter and give it a tail one space long.

Watch how the children join the two strokes. When there is a tail on a letter, the children are not likely to be as careful in joining the strokes accurately as when the strokes stop at the junction. **The strokes should neither gap nor overlap.**

Watch the length of the tail of the letter. Be sure the children are making it one space long, but **not all the way to the top line** of the next row.

Be sure the children have **good alignment** with this letter. The **tops of the strokes must be at the middle line.** The junction of the two strokes should be right at the bottom line, not above or below it.

Lesson 32
The Letter z

Lesson 32

The Letter z

buzz

zoo   zip

y

69

Aim of the Lesson

To teach the manuscript letter *z*.

Directions

The children should trace over the strokes and letters in row one. The letter *z* should be practiced in row two. In row three they should trace over the words *zoo* and *zip* and then use the rest of the space to practice the letter *z*. Row four is a review of the letter *y*. It should be traced over and copied to the end of the row.

Conducting the Class

Ask these questions in relation to the picture:

"What kind of noise does a bee make when it flies?" (Probably the children will say "Zzzz" or "Humm.")

"If we want a word that tells us the noise a bee makes when it flies, what would we say?" ("Buzz.")

"What might be one reason God makes bees buzz when they fly?" (To tell us they are near so that we do not get stung.)

Have the children **trace over the dotted letters** in the word *buzz*. **Ask the children:**

"What stroke does the letter *z* **have that the letter** *e* **also has?"** (An across line.)

"The letter *e* is the only letter previous to this one that has an **across line. Suppose we practice this line** just a little to help us in making the letter *z*." (They may practice either on paper or on the board.)

"How many **strokes does the letter** *z* **have?" (Three.)** Have one of the children look at the letter and call out the names of all the strokes.

Demonstrate the formation of the letter as you **explain** it:

"The first stroke of this letter is an across line that runs along the middle line. It should be the same distance across as the height of one space. At the end of the across line, do not lift your pencil but **make a forward-slanting line.** It should aim for the bottom line at a point straight below the beginning of the across line. Stop when you get to the bottom line, and **make an across line again** in the same direction as the first line. It should stop at a point straight down from the end of the first across line."

Have the children practice at the blackboard and then pro-ceed with the lesson according to the directions.

Further Helps for the Teacher

Watch that the forward-slanting line does not become either too steep or too slanted. This is one of the major problems children have in forming this letter correctly. It is a result of not aiming carefully enough for the point directly beneath the beginning of the across stroke. If any have a problem with this, you may need to draw dotted lines down both sides of their letters so that they know just where each line is to begin and end.

Another important item to check is **the length of the across lines.** Be sure that they are not too short or too long. They should be approximately **one-half inch.**

Check again on the **posture and pencil-holding habits** of your children. These will quickly deteriorate unless you remind your children of them often.

Keep a check on the review line in each lesson. It can be a test of whether the children really have learned the letter from the previous lesson.

Lesson 33
The Numeral 7

Lesson 33

The Numeral 7

7 7 7 7 7 7 7 7 7

September						
Sun.	Mon.	Tue.	Wed.	Thur.	Fri.	Sat.
	1	2	3	4	5	6
7	8	9	10	11	12	13
14	15	16	17	18	19	20
21	22	23	24	25	26	27
28	29	30				

79   box

z

71

Aim of the Lesson

To teach the numeral 7.

Directions

The children should trace over the strokes and numerals in row one. In row two the numeral 7 should be practiced. In row three they should trace over the number *79* and the word *box* and then use the rest of the row to practice the numeral 7. Row four is a review of the letter *z*. The letter should be traced over and copied to the end of the row.

Conducting the Class

Ask these questions in relation to the picture:

"How many days are in a week?" (Seven.)

"Do we work every day of the week?" (No; one day out of seven we rest and worship God.)

"What day do we use for rest and worship?" (Sunday.)

If the children do not understand the calendar as drawn in the picture, you do not need to go into detail. The important thing is to associate the numeral 7 with the seven days of the week.

Demonstrate and **explain** the formation of the numeral 7. **Begin by showing the similarities and differences between the numeral 7 and the letter** *z*. The **numeral 7 is two spaces high,** whereas the letter *z* is only one space high. The numeral 7 **has only two strokes;** the letter *z* has three strokes. The **numeral 7 does not have the last across line (on the bottom)** as does the letter *z*.

The **across line in the numeral 7** is made in the same direction as the across line of the letter *z*, but it **runs along the top line** rather than the middle line. **It is also a little longer** than the across line of the letter *z*. Do not lift the pencil at the end of the across line, but go on and **make the forward-slanting line.** This line is drawn **all the way to the bottom line.** It does not slant quite as much as the forward-slanting line of the letter; but when it reaches the bottom line, it must be **straight below the beginning** of the first stroke of the numeral.

Following explanation, demonstration, and **blackboard practice,** have the children **proceed with the lesson** according to the directions.

Further Helps for the Teacher

If you have time, give your children some **blackboard review of the manuscript strokes and a few of the letters,** especially **from the previous sections.** If you do this, review will not take as much time in the next lesson.

Be sure the children are drawing *straight lines.* **A long line has a tendency to wiggle.** Watch the **angle of the slanted line** (see fourth paragraph under "Conducting the Class") and the **length of the across line.** With this numeral, it should be about five-eighths inch long.

Lesson 34
Review of Slant-stroke Letters

Lesson 34

Review of Slant-stroke Letters

W   7

k   V

X   y

Z

73

Aim of the Lesson

To thoroughly review the letters *k, v, w, x, y, z,* and the numeral 7. A less extensive review will be given to the letters learned previously.

Directions

In each row that begins with a letter or numeral, the children are to trace over each figure and copy it to the end of the space provided. In the last half row, the teacher is to call out the manuscript strokes (with the exception of the large circle and curve strokes), and the children are to draw one of each in the space provided.

Conducting the Class

Explain to the children: "This is **a review of the last seven letters** and numerals you have learned. What do we call these letters? How are they different from the other letters and numerals we have learned?"

Give the names of all the letters and numerals learned in this section and place them on the blackboard in plain view of all. Call the children to the board (if a small class), or give them a piece of writing paper.

Ask them these questions and have them write down their answers:

"Which letters or numerals are made up of only slanting lines?" (*v, w, x, y.*)

"Which letters or numerals have no backward-slanting lines?" (*z, 7.*)

"Which letters or numerals have both forward- and backward-slanting lines?" (*k, v, w, x, y.*)

"Which letter or numeral has two backward-slanting and two forward-slanting lines?" (*w.*)

"Which letter or numeral contains a down line?" (*k.*)

"Which letters or numerals have across lines?" (*z, 7.*)

Following this drill, on the board **review with the children the letters** from the previous sections **that are not reviewed in Lesson 34.**

Further Helps for the Teacher

Are your children still meeting the goals outlined in Lessons 8, 14, and 26? As you review the letters learned in previous sections, you should be keeping these goals in mind.

In addition to these, **your children should have achieved the following goals** in the last seven lessons:

1. They should be able to understand and put into practice the **principles of letter formation for the seven letters and numerals** they have just finished learning. This includes—
   a. a fair amount of **accuracy in making slant strokes** with the correct degree of slant for each particular letter;
   b. having the **ability to join slant strokes** without gap or overlap, especially in the letters *k* and *y*.

2. The children should be **improving their alignment** of letters. They should be learning to stop their strokes promptly at the lines, not above or below them.

3. They should be **improving in their ability to make straight lines** straight. Smoothness, not jerkiness and waviness, should characterize their lines.

For your quick reference, **here are the slant-stroke letters** with the strokes in the order in which they are composed:

k—down line, forward-slanting (f-s) line, backward-slanting (b-s) line

v—b-s line, f-s line

w—b-s line, f-s line, b-s line, f-s line

x—b-s line, f-s line

y—b-s line, f-s line

z—across line, f-s line, across line

7—across line, f-s line

Lesson 35
The Letter c

Lesson 35

The Letter c

c c c c c c c c c c | coat

cat back

7

75

Aim of the Lesson

To teach the manuscript letter *c*.

Directions

Have the children trace over the letters in row one. In row two they should practice the letter *c*. In row three the children are to trace over the words *cat* and *back* and then practice *c* in the rest of the row. Row four is a review of the numeral 7. The children should trace over it and copy it to the end of the row.

Conducting the Class

Ask the children these questions in relation to the picture:
"What do you see in the picture?" (A coat.)
"How many of you have a coat?"
"When do you wear a coat?" (When going outside on cold days.)
"Why is a coat necessary?" (To keep us warm when it is cold.)
Explain to the children that some children's parents do not have money to buy coats that are heavy enough to keep them warm. They may shiver most of the winter, while we are comfortable. If God has given us a heavy coat to keep us warm in the cold, we should be thankful for it and be glad to wear it when we are told.

Have the children **trace over the dotted letter** c in the word *coat*: **Begin by discussing curve strokes,** which the children are to begin using with this lesson. **Let them practice the curve** before beginning to master the letter c, **so that they can regain the feel** of the stroke.

Ask the children if they can remember **a letter they have already learned that was made with a curve.** It was included with the circle letters because it is a very important and frequently used letter. It is **the letter** e. The part circle (curve) in the letter e makes almost a complete circle. Have the children **practice the letter** e several times.

The letter c **is made very much like the letter** e. Explain its formation as follows:

"Begin making the letter c about the same place that you learned to begin making the small circle. **Begin** just **a short distance below the middle line** and **toward the right side** of the letter. Make the letter c just as you would make a circle, but do not come all the way back to the beginning. **Stop your circle about the same distance from the bottom line as you began it from the top line.** When you are finished, your letter should look like a circle with a small space erased."

Following the above explanation and **blackboard practice,** have the children **proceed with the lesson** according to the directions.

Further Helps for the Teacher

It will probably be easier for your children to draw complete circles accurately than it will be for them to draw a part circle the nature of the letter c. Draw their attention back to the fact that **the letter** c

must have the *shape* **of a circle,** even though it does not make a complete one. The children at first may make their *c*'s **too narrow,** and the curve of the letter will probably be noticeably sharper at some places than others. It will likely be some time before your children will be able to make a properly curved *c* to your satisfaction. Do not be discouraged with them, but continue correcting and reminding them until they can make the letter correctly. Be sure to commend their efforts when they succeed.

Lesson 36
The Letter u

Lesson 36

The Letter u

up

quick

77

Aim of the Lesson

To teach the manuscript letter *u*.

Directions

The children should trace over the strokes and letters in row one. In row two the children should practice the letter *u*. In row three the children should trace the word *quick* and then use the rest of the row to practice *u*. Row four is a review of the letter *c*. It should be traced over and copied to the end of the row.

Conducting the Class

Ask the children these questions in relation to the picture:

"In what direction is the man pointing?" (Up.)

"What things can you think of that are up?" (The sky, clouds, birds, trees, stars, sun, moon, tops of tall buildings, heaven, God.) Have the children **trace over the dotted letter** in the word *up*.

Demonstrate the letter *u* on the blackboard, explaining its formation at the same time. Since the children are not familiar with this type of curve stroke (small half-circle) **within** a letter, be especially careful in demonstrating to be sure the children understand each stroke as it is given. Explain the letter in the following manner:

"The letter *u* **is a four-stroke letter**. [Let the children try to pick out the strokes.] It is also a short letter, so it **must stay between the bottom and middle lines.** The whole letter is drawn without lifting your pencil.

"The first stroke is **a down line** beginning at the middle line and going down. But it only goes **partway** to the bottom line. Before getting there, **a curve is begun.** It curves **around to the right,** touches the bottom line, and curves up again. It then changes to **an up line** [like a down line, except it starts at the bottom and goes up], which goes back up **to the middle line. The fourth stroke is a down line.** It starts down along the third stroke and goes **straight down to the bottom line,** thus finishing the letter."

Have the children do considerable practice of this letter at the blackboard. Use the guidelines under **"Further Helps for the Teacher"** to help you help them.

Following the above explanation and practice, have the children **proceed with the lesson** according to the directions. Check on **posture and pencil-holding** habits, and supervise them carefully.

Further Helps for the Teacher

You will want to be sure your children are using **the right size curve** in making the letter *u*. In order to give the letter *u* the proper shape, the diameter of the curve should be smaller than that used for the letters *c* and *e*.

Some children may **tend to give the curve something other than a true part-circle appearance.** For example, some children **may come down too far with their first and third strokes,** leaving room in the second stroke for only a very small rounded corner on each side and straight line across the bottom (⊔). Or **they may not curve fast enough,** giving the letter too much point at the bottom (∪).

Although **the up and down lines should blend** to a certain extent **with the curve,** you must **be sure they do not become a part of the curve.** There should be distinct up and down lines that are plainly noticeable, like this (∪), not like this (∪).

Be sure the final stroke of the letter retraces the third stroke accurately. It should not deviate from the third stroke until it meets the curve. At that point it should deviate promptly and continue straight down to the bottom line.

Lesson 37
The Letter r

Lesson 37

The Letter r

r r r r r r r r r r work

rat rug

u

79

Aim of the Lesson

To teach the manuscript letter *r*.

Directions

The children should trace over the letters in row one. Row two is for practice of the letter *r*. In row three, they should trace over the words *rat* and *rug* and then use the rest of the row to practice the letter *r*. Row four is a review of the letter *u*. It should be traced over and then copied to the end of the row.

Conducting the Class

Ask the children these questions in relation to the picture:

"What is the girl in the picture doing?" (Sweeping the steps.)

"Did your parents ever ask you to sweep the steps?"

Explain to the children that sweeping the steps is one way of working. Children can work at other things as well. God is pleased when children work cheerfully without grumbling.

Have the children **trace over the dotted letter in the word** *work*.

Briefly **discuss the letter** *r* with the children. Tell the children to turn their pages upside-down and look at the letter. What does it look like? It looks like the letter *u* without its first stroke.

Demonstrate the letter **while explaining** its formation as follows:

"Is this letter a tall letter or a short letter?" (Short.) "Since it is a **short letter,** it **must stay between the bottom and middle lines.** The **first stroke is a down line** that goes straight from the middle line to the bottom line. The **second stroke is an up line** that goes partway back up to the middle line. It must stop in time to leave room for the **third stroke, a curve.** It curves around to the right, touches the middle line, and curves back down again. The letter is finished. **The words** *down, up,* **and** *around* **describe how this letter is made.**"

Following the above explanation and demonstration, have the children come to the **blackboard** and **practice** the letter. Before they practice the letter as a whole, **have them practice it in a step-by-step manner,** practicing each stroke separately and then putting the strokes together to make a whole letter.

Send the children to their seats and have them **proceed with the lesson** according to the directions.

Further Helps for the Teacher

Some children may have difficulty beginning their curves at the right place on the stem. **They may begin their curves too early,** some even beginning to curve a little right from the bottom. This, of course, ruins the appearance of the letter. Do not allow your children to make the letter in this lazy way.

Some also may begin the curve too near the middle line to make a really good curve and stay below the middle line. A child who does this has two alternatives: he may overstep the middle line, and thus the letter will fail in alignment; or he may stay below the line and just go straight out from the stem before curving down. Either error will produce a letter with a poor appearance. So be sure to **teach carefully the proper place of beginning for the curve.**

The children should put plenty of practice into this letter, until you are satisfied that they are able to make the letter properly. **Do not forget the practice lines on the back of each lesson page.** Be sure the children have learned to form each letter well before moving on to the next one.

Lesson 38
The Letter n

Lesson 38

The Letter n

night

no not

r

81

Aim of the Lesson

To teach the manuscript letter *n*.

Directions

The children should trace over the strokes and letters in row one. In row two they should practice the letter *n*. The two words in row three should be traced over and the rest of the space used to practice the letter *n*. Row four is a review of the letter *r*. That letter should be traced over and copied to the end of the row.

Conducting the Class

Ask the children these questions in relation to the picture:

"Do children need to be afraid if nighttime?" (No.)

"Why not?" (Because God can take care of us just as well at night as in the daytime.)

Have the children **trace over the dotted letter** n in the word *night*.

Look with the children at **the letter** n. **Turn the letter upside-down** as you did the letter r. With this letter the children should very quickly be able to pick out the letter u, since the letter n is the exact opposite of that letter.

Compare the letter n **with the letter** r. Ask the children to explain to you how the letter n is different from the letter r. If they cannot immediately think of the difference, have them look at the first four figures in row one. Ask them, "Which one looks like the letter r?" (The third one.) **"What was done to the letter** r **to make the letter** n **in the next figure?"** (A down line was added to the end of the curve.)

While the similarity of the letter r to the letter n is fresh on the children's minds, begin a **demonstration** and **explanation** of the letter:

"Beginning at the middle line, we make **a down line** that goes to the bottom line (just like the letter r). **For the second stroke,** we make **an up line,** which goes partway back up to the middle line. Before it gets there, it changes to a curve, which curves forward, touches the middle line and then curves down again. At the end of the curve we make a down line, which goes to the bottom line."

Teach your children the following description of the letter n: **down, up, around, down.** Have them practice the letter as you repeat the description.

Following **blackboard practice,** have the children **proceed with the lesson** according to the directions. Supervise them carefully, keeping watch on their **posture and pencil-holding** habits.

Further Helps for the Teacher

Be sure the children understand that **the curve of this letter,** as well as of the letter r, **is made forward,** not backward. With a letter of this nature, in which it is possible to curve either way, some children may become confused.

Do not neglect to compare this letter with previous letters mentioned in this lesson. One principle of learning is that one needs to build upon what has been previously learned. An effective wall cannot be laid unless there are previously laid blocks upon which to lay the next row of blocks. The same holds true in penmanship.

All the **helps given for the letter r will also apply in this lesson.** In addition, you will need to watch these areas:

1. **The end points of the curve line should be directly a cross from each other.**
2. **The curve should be well rounded, without points.**
3. The children's **letters should not be squeezed too tightly together** nor **spread** too far apart.
4. The children's **up and down lines should be straight** and **not blended too much with the curve line.** There must be a distinction between the curve line and each straight line that joins it.

Lesson 39
The Letter m

Lesson 39

The Letter m

i l r n n n m m m | smile

my man

n

83

Aim of the Lesson

To teach the manuscript letter *m*.

Directions

The children should trace over the strokes and letters in row one. Row two is for practice. In row three they should trace over the words *my* and *man* and use the rest of the row to practice the letter *m*. Row four is a review of the letter *n*. The letter should be traced over and copied to the end of the row.

Conducting the Class

Ask the children these questions in relation to the picture:

"When a person is smiling, what does it usually mean?" (He is happy.)

"Does it also make others happy when you smile?" (Yes.)

"Why should children be happy and have smiling faces?" (Because God has given them so things to enjoy.)

Have the children **trace over the dotted letter** *m* in the word *smile*.

In looking at the letter *m*, one should quite readily notice that **the letter *m* is very closely related to the letter** *n*. Basically, it is a double *n*. The second hump is what changes the letter *n* into the letter *m*. If the many strokes of the letter confuse the children, this simple fact may help them.

After you have discussed the appearance of the letter *m*, **demonstrate it** on the board, explaining it in the following manner:

"Beginning at the middle line, draw **a down line** to the bottom line. Draw **an up line** along the first line toward the middle line. Before reaching the middle line, begin **a curve line** forward up to the middle line and down again. Now make the **fourth and fifth strokes, simply going down to the bottom line and right back up again.** The **sixth stroke is another curve forward and up** to the middle line and then down again. The **seventh stroke is a down line** that goes to the bottom line, finishing the letter."

The above detailed explanation will of course confuse the children unless you are demonstrating the letter. To help the children remember the formation of the letter, **teach them this simple description of the letter: down, up, around, down, up, around, down.** As with the letter *n*, have them practice as you call the strokes.

Following **blackboard practice,** have the children **proceed with the lesson** according to the directions. **Supervise** their work carefully, and keep check on their **posture and pencil-holding habits.**

Further Helps for the Teacher

Since the letter *m* is made in a manner similar to the letter *n*, many of the problems associated with the two letters will be the same.

Also, there may be a tendency to have **inconsistent spacing between the legs of the letter.** This may be a result of a lack of carefulness in making the curves. Encourage your children to be sure they are making their curves the same size. **A failure to make straight up and down lines** will also cause this problem.

In this letter there are two places where up and down lines retrace each other for a distance. **Be sure this retracing is accurately done.**

With this letter, again **continue to help your children to make well-rounded, distinct curves,** blended enough with the up and down lines that there is no point between the two, yet not so much that it makes the up and down lines curved or the curve lines straight. You will no doubt need to slow some of your children down in their writing to accomplish this.

Carefulness in making this letter **will solve many problems** before they arise.

Lesson 40
The Letter h

Lesson 40

The Letter h

h h h h h h h h h h h

hide

he him

m

85

Aim of the Lesson

To teach the manuscript letter *h*.

Directions

The children should trace over the strokes and letters in row one. They should practice the letter *h* in row two. In row three they should trace over the words *he* and *him,* using the rest of the row to practice the letter *h*. Row four is a review of the letter *m*. It should be traced over and copied to the end of the row.

Conducting the Class

Ask these questions in relation to the picture:

"What is the girl in the picture trying to do?" (Hide.)

"Why do you think she is hiding?" (Possibilities—she may be playing hide-and-seek, or she may be hiding from her mother so that she does not have to do something she does not want to do.)

"Even though the girl may think she can hide from her mother, who can't she hide from?" (God, because He can see everyone all the time.)

Have the children **trace over the dotted letter** h in the word *hide*.

Let the children share their ideas about the letter h. **Ask them to tell you which other letter this one resembles most.** If they cannot guess that it looks like the letter n, they will quickly if you erase the top part of the stem of the letter.

Explain to the children that **the only difference between the letter** h **and the letter** n is that in the letter h, the first stroke, which is a down line, is drawn all the way from the top line instead of starting at the middle line. The **letter** h **is made up of four strokes,** just like the letter n.

Go through an explanation of the strokes as you demonstrate on the board. The letter h begins with **a down line drawn from the top line to the bottom line.** The **second stroke is an up line,** which retraces the first stroke partway back up toward the middle line. Here the **third stroke, a curve,** begins, curving forward up to the middle line and then back down until it is directly across from its beginning. From there the **fourth stroke, a down line,** is drawn to the bottom line.

Give the children **practice at the blackboard** and then have them **proceed with the lesson** according to the directions.

Further Helps for the Teacher

Be sure when your children draw this letter, that **they make the down line truly vertical,** not slanted.

Observe whether they are **making their curves accurately.** The top of the curve should just touch the middle line and not drop below or rise above it. The highest point of the curve should be equidistant from both sides.

See that the children **retrace accurately with the second stroke.** There should be no space at all between the first and second strokes, and no curve at all in the second stroke.

120

Lesson 41
The Letter f

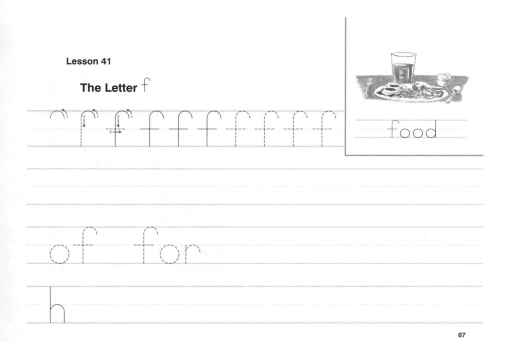

Lesson 41

The Letter f

food

of for

h

87

Aim of the Lesson

To teach the manuscript letter *f*.

Directions

The children should trace over the strokes and letters in row one. In row two they should practice the letter *f*. In row three they should trace over the words *of* and *for*, using the rest of the space to practice the letter *f*. Row four is a review of the letter *h*. The children should trace over and copy it to the end of the row.

Conducting the Class

Ask the children these questions in relation to the picture:

"What do you see in the picture that you should be thankful for?" (Food.)

"Is it right to complain about the food that God has given you?" (No, it is not right.)

Have the children **trace over the dotted letter** *f* in the word *food*.

As you look at the letter *f,* explain to the children that the **shape of this letter is entirely different** from any curve letters that they have learned so far. In some ways, it is like **the letter** *t*, but not in every way. **Ask the children to tell you how the two letters are different.** (The letter *f* has a curve at the top. The down line of the letter *f* does not begin at the top line. The "cross" of the letter *f* crosses on the middle line, not some distance above the line as with the letter *t*.)

Explain and **demonstrate** the letter *f* on the blackboard by **discussing it in a manner similar to the following:**

"Is the letter *f* a tall or a short letter" (Tall.) **"How many strokes** make up the letter *f*?" **(Three.)** "The **first stroke is a curve.** The curve **begins a short distance below the top line** and curves backward, up to the top line, and down again. **When the curve is finished, a down line is drawn** from the end of it to the bottom line. At this point your pencil is lifted, and **the stem is crossed at the middle line with an across line** about the same length as the 'cross' on the letter *t*."

To help the children remember the formation of the letter, **teach them this description of the letter: around, down, (lift), across.**

Following the above explanation, demonstration, and **blackboard practice,** have the children **proceed with the lesson** according to the directions. Supervise carefully, checking on **posture and pencil holding.**

Further Helps for the Teacher

In demonstrating and teaching this letter, you will notice that the **curve line is made from right to left** rather than from left to right. This should not be too difficult for your children, since when they learned the curve line, they practiced it going both ways. But if you feel they lack in this area, you should give the children **extra practice** in making the curve line going from right to left.

The **children may have a problem in knowing just where to begin** the curve line. With careful demonstration and explanation, you can help your children get started right. Be sure that they start the letter far enough forward so as to leave adequate space between it and the previous letter, even though at first it may seem like too much space.

Be sure the curve has a good part-circle shape. It should be started *well below* the top line. The tendency may be to start fairly near the top line, thereby making the curve too shallow.

Again, **be sure the children are joining the curve line and the down line correctly.** The down line should not be a part of the curve line, nor the curve line part of the down line.

Some children may get **the letter *t* and the letter *f* mixed up in relation to where the across line is to be placed.** Emphasize that the across line of the letter *f* is to cross the down line *right at* the middle line.

Lesson 42
The Letter j

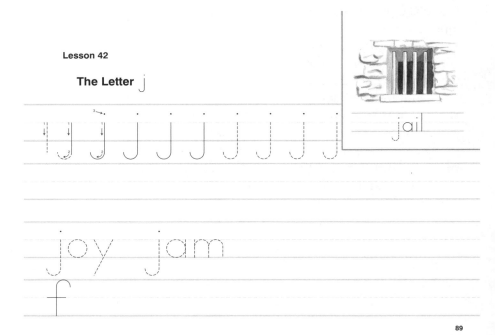

Lesson 42

The Letter j

jail

joy jam

f

89

Aim of the Lesson

To teach the manuscript letter *j*.

Directions

The children should trace over the strokes and letters in row one. In row two they should practice the letter. In row three they should trace over the words *joy* and *jam*, using the rest of the space to practice the letter *f*. Row four is a review of the letter *f*. It should be traced over and copied to the end of the row.

Conducting the Class

Ask the children these questions in relation to the picture.

"What kind of building has bars in the windows?" (A jail.)

"Why does it have bars?" (So no one who is put there can get out.)

"What kind of people are usually put in jail?" (Those who disobey the law.)

Explain to the children that those who do what is right usually do not get put into jail, but it is those who do wrong.

Have the children **trace over the dotted letter** *j* in the word *jail*.

As an introduction to the **letter** *j,* **compare it with the letter** *f.* Have the children write the letter *f* and then turn their papers **upside-down.** They will see that the basic structure is the same. One primary difference is that the letter *j* begins at a different place than the letter *f*.

Explain and demonstrate the formation of the letter. Ask the children, **"How many different strokes** makeup this letter?" (**Three.**) Have one or more of the children point these out to you. They are a **down line, a curve, and a dot.** The children should be experienced enough by now in the formation of letters that **they can guess at the order of strokes** in this letter. Have them help you make the letter by telling you which stroke to make at what time.

To form this letter, **begin at the middle line and make a down line.** This line goes **below the bottom line** about as far as the line of the letter *g*. Then **make a backward curve beginning at the end of this line. Finally, a dot** is placed above the stem of the letter just as in the letter *i*.

After you have explained the lesson as outlined above, have the children come to the **blackboard** and **practice** the letter. They should then **proceed with the lesson** according to the directions. Be sure they are putting to practice what they know about **good posture** and **correct pencil holding.**

Further Helps for the Teacher

It may be **easy** for your children **to crowd this letter,** because its beginning stroke is on the right side of the letter. A crowded *j* will probably produce a curve that is too deep and not wide enough (**j**). So be sure the children begin far enough to the right to give them adequate space to make a proper curve.

One of the most frequent errors encountered in making the letter *j* is the **tendency to blend the down line and the curve together into one large curve,** especially below the bottom line (*j*). Insist that the children do not begin the curve until the down line is first brought down far enough.

There may also be a **tendency to vary the length of the letter below the line.** Watch that the bottom of the letter is the proper distance below the line and also that it is well aligned with every other letter *j* in the row. Work for consistency in this area.

Be sure also that **the dot of the letter is the right distance above the top** of the letter. It must not be carelessly positioned to one side of the letter or the other. Teach your children the habit of placing their dots accurately from the beginning, and it may avoid carelessness in this area in later years.

Lesson 43
The Letter s

Lesson 43

The Letter s

s s s s s s s s s s s s

song

is so say

j

91

Aim of the Lesson

To teach the manuscript letter *s*.

Directions

The letters and strokes in row one should be traced over. In row two the children should practice the letter. In row three they should trace over the words *is, so,* and *say* and then use the rest of the row to practice the letter *s*. Row four is a review of the letter *j*. The children should trace over it and then copy it to the end of the row.

Conducting the Class

Ask the children these questions in relation to the picture:

"What do you see in the picture?" (Part of a song.)

"When do we sing songs?" (At church, at home, at school.)

"What do we use to sing?" (Our voices—see Lesson 28.)

Explain to the children that when we sing songs, we are praising God. Have the children **trace over the dotted letter** *s* in the word *song*.

The letter *s* **is one of the odd letters of the alphabet.** It is more difficult to see how it conforms to the rules. But if we look at it very carefully, we will see that it does.

Explain to the children that the letter *s* **is made up of two curves that go in** *different* **directions.** We call them **"double curves."** Ask the children, "If two curves were put together going the same direction, what would we have?" (A circle. Demonstrate if necessary.) But when we put them together going different directions, we have made the letter *s*.

Explain and demonstrate in detail the formation of the letter, as follows:

"This letter is **one space high.** It must stay between the middle line and the bottom line. The **first stroke** of the letter **begins on the forward side** of the letter, **a short distance below the middle line. From the beginning point**, it curves around up to the middle line and back down again. It continues curving until the curve is going in about the same direction as the middle line. [Note that these curves are just slightly longer than they are round.] At this point, **we begin curving in the other direction to make the second curve.** It curves down toward the bottom line. The curve should touch the bottom line as it goes around, and then curve back up a short distance. The letter stops about the same distance above the bottom line as it began below the middle line."

Following this explanation and demonstration, **the children should practice double curving in the air so that they get the feel** of the double curve. As they come to the **blackboard,** begin by having them **practice** the double curve fairly rapidly on the board. Then work at the letter more precisely for accuracy. As the **children do their lesson**, be on hand to insure that they are making the letter accurately and maintaining **carefulness in posture and pencil holding.**

Further Helps for the Teacher

Most letters with curves also have straight lines that help to "support" the curves. But the letter *s* **is nothing but curves. This will make accuracy with this letter more difficult for your children.** Straight lines, whether vertical, horizontal, or slanted, are simpler to form than curves because the perfect standard can be more easily visualized in the mind. Even circles can be more easily visualized than curves. So do not be surprised if your children come up with a letter that is out of shape **the first few times. The letter may be too wide or too narrow, curves may be out of balance up and down, the curves themselves or the joining of the two curves may be inaccurate,** or **the letter may be slanted** one way or the other. But do not become discouraged and "accept the inevitable." Your children *can* learn to make this letter correctly. It will take much practice on their part (do not forget the practice lines on the reverse side of their lesson page) and careful supervision on your part. It may be necessary to re-explain the formation of the letter to individual children. Emphasize that really the letter s **is no more than two part circles facing opposite directions, placed one above the other and joined in the middle.**

The letter should be made **straight enough that a vertical line could be drawn down each side of the letter,** touching two points on the letter.

Be sure no one is **making the letter backward (2).** This type of letter is sometimes confusing in this respect. But that can be helped if the children remember to start it the same direction as the *c* and *f*.

Spacing could be a problem with this letter, since the first stroke is begun on the forward side of the letter (see Lesson 41).

Lesson 44
The Numeral 2

Lesson 44

The Numeral 2

2 2 2 2 2 2 2 2

12 21 72

S

93

Aim of the Lesson

To teach the numeral 2.

Directions

The strokes and numerals in row one are to be traced over. In row two the children should practice the numeral 2. The numbers *12, 21,* and *72* in row three should be traced over and the rest of the row used practice the numeral 2. Row four is a review of the letter *s*. It should be traced over and copied to the end of the row.

Conducting the Class

Ask the children these questions in relation to the picture:

"How many hands do you have?" (Two.)

"Could you get along with one hand just as well as with two?" (No.)

"What are some good things for you to do with your hands?"

Explain to the children that God wants us to do things that are good and helpful with our hands, not things that are wrong.

Discuss the general appearance of the numeral 2 with the children. Ask them, "Can you think of any other letter or numeral that looks somewhat like the numeral 2?" (Discuss how the letters they suggest compare with the numeral 2.)

Explain that **the numeral 2 does not actually look very much like other letters and numerals.** No other letter or numeral is made exactly the same way. Have the **children name the strokes of this numeral** if they can. The **three** strokes are: a **curve**, a **forward-slanting line,** and an **across line.**

Demonstrate this numeral while explaining its formation as follows:

"The first stroke, which is a curve, begins just below the top line. It curves up to the top line and then down and around until it has almost reached the middle line. By this time it is starting to curve backward. Stop curving and **begin drawing a forward-slanting line to the bottom line.** Without lifting your pencil, **draw an across line.** Draw it long enough that **it will end directly beneath the outer part of the curve."**

The children should **practice** the numeral 2 **on the blackboard,** while the explanation is still fresh in their minds. After they have done so, give them some extra practice in some other letters in this section that may be difficult for some of them. After blackboard practice, the children should go to their seats and **proceed with the lesson** while you supervise their work. Watch their **position and pencil holding,** and correct if necessary.

Further Helps for the Teacher

This is the **first time** the children have learned a figure that contains a **tilted curve and a slanted line joined together.** This **combination may be confusing.** If they have a problem with this, draw the individual strokes on the board separately, talk about each one, and have the children draw each stroke separately in its correct position on the lines. Then have them put the three strokes together to make the numeral.

The children will probably have **more difficulty with the curve than with any other part of this numeral.** The normal curve problems will likely appear—**irregular** curving, **points on the curve,** curves **too shallow** or **too narrow and deep.** The **size** of the curve is also important with this numeral. The curve should have a good part-*circle* appearance. With children who have difficulty getting a well-rounded curve in this numeral, have them draw a circle and then erase the half they do not need before proceeding with the rest of the letter. Use this exercise for practice only.

Train your children to draw their curves rather rapidly. It is **almost impossible to draw a smooth curve slowly.** It will be easier for your children to correct a curve error while writing more rapidly than while writing tediously slow.

Insist upon a *straight* **line for the slanting line.** As speed is picked up, some children may want to draw one big gentle curve to replace both the curve and the slanting line. Be sure all the curve stays in the curve and does not continue into the slanting line.

Be sure the slanting line is made at the proper angle. The slanting line should be aimed for a point on the line farther back than the beginning of the curve line above (*2*). This gives the numeral *2* a more balanced appearance.

The **length of the across line** must also be watched. The across line should stop directly below the point *farthest to the right* on the curve at the top (*2*).

Lesson 45
The Numeral 3

Lesson 45

The Numeral 3

95

Aim of the Lesson

To teach the numeral *3*.

Directions

The children should trace over the strokes and numerals in row one. Row two is for practice of the numeral. In row three the children should trace over each number and use the rest of the row to practice the numeral *3*. Row four is a review of the numeral *2*. The children should trace over and copy it to the end of the row.

133

Conducting the Class

Ask the children these questions in relation to the picture:

"How many kinds of lights has God put in the sky?" (Three.)

"What are their names?" (Sun, moon, and stars.)

"Which light shines during the day?" (Sun.)

"Which lights shine at night?" (The moon and stars.)

Demonstrate and **explain** the formation of the numeral *3*. To help the children understand the formation better, ask them a number of leading questions given in a logical order, utilizing the information given in the following paragraph. (Examples: "How tall is the numeral *3*?" "How many strokes are in the numeral *3*?" "What kind of strokes are they?" "Are there any straight lines?")

The numeral *3* is made up of **two curves, one above the other.** The **first stroke of the numeral** *3* **begins just below the top line,** curves up to the top line, and then down around and back along the middle line. When the first curve has reached its bottom at the middle line, the second curve begins. **At the middle line the second curve retraces the first for a very short distance** while curving down and around to the bottom line. From the bottom line, curve up a short distance so that the end of the numeral is directly below the beginning of the numeral.

The **children should draw the numeral in the air several times** before practicing it. They should also be given some **blackboard practice** before **proceeding with the lesson. Supervise** their work and keep check on their **position and pencil holding.**

Further Helps for the Teacher

The curves of the numeral *3* **are not half-circles.** They are somewhat larger, making a curve about the size of **five-eighths of a circle.** The extra one-eighth of a circle is added at the beginning and the end of the numeral. Draw a straight line up and down at the end of the junction of the two curves to help you understand this (3). Do not try to explain these fractional relationships to the children, but understanding them yourself will help you to help your children in getting this numeral well proportioned and accurate.

The numeral *3,* **like the letter** *s,* **has no straight lines to help the children guide the straightness of the figure.** So artificial guidelines will need to be used. **For those whose figures tend to**

be crooked, draw dotted vertical lines the right distance apart on their papers, asking them to draw the numeral 3 within those two lines, touching them at two points on each side (3). You can also use the straight dotted line to show up any crookedness in numerals that have been already made.

Watch how the two strokes are joined. They should only retrace each other for a very short distance before they begin curving in opposite directions. Some children may run the strokes together for too great a distance, thereby extending the middle point out too far, sometimes even as far as the beginning and ending points of the numeral (3). Some children may not allow the two curves to run together at all (3). This will eventually produce a nearly illegible numeral.

Again, the curve must be accurately and smoothly made. Set your standard for a well-made curve, and hold the children to it.

Remember, time spent under supervised practice is time well spent.

Lesson 46
The Numeral 5

Lesson 46

The Numeral 5

5 5 5 5 5 5 5 5 5

15 25 35

3

Aim of the Lesson

To teach the numeral 5.

Directions

The children should trace over the strokes and numerals in row one. The numeral 5 should be practiced in row two. In row three the numbers 15, 25, and 35 should be traced over and the rest of the space used to practice the numeral 5. Row four is a review of the numeral 3. The children should trace over and copy it to the end of the row.

Conducting the Class

Ask the children these questions in relation to the picture:

"In the last lesson how many hands did you say that you have?" (Two.)

"What do we call the parts of the hand that we use to hold a pencil?" (Fingers.)

"How many fingers do you have on each hand?" (Five.)

"What are some things that you can do with your fingers?" (Write, pick up small things, stop leaks, and so forth.)

Tell the children that today they are going to learn to print the numeral that tells us how many fingers we have on each hand.

Place the numeral 5 on the blackboard, taking care that the children **do not see it being made. Let the children tell you where they think the numeral was begun.** Unless they have previously been taught this numeral, their answer will likely be that the numeral began with the across line at the top. To draw their attention to this very common error, have them continue guessing which is the proper place to begin the numeral. **If they cannot guess, tell them the right answer** (that the top of the forward-slanting line is the place to begin). Then move on into the following **explanation, progressively moving your demonstration along** with the explanation. Give the explanation in your own words, mixing the explanation with questions to keep the children's attention.

The **numeral 5 is a three-stroke numeral,** which begins at the top line. **The first stroke is a forward-slanting line** (it slants forward only a little). It is drawn from the top line down below the middle line. Here it stops promptly and **the second stroke begins. It is a curve** that curves up and forward. The **top part of the curve goes above the middle line.** It continues curving around and down on the forward side to touch the bottom line, finally curving up a little to give the numeral a short tail. The **pencil is then lifted** and placed at the top of the forward-slanting line **to begin the third stroke, an across line.** This line stops directly above the edge of the curve.

Have the children **practice the numeral in the air and on the blackboard.** After you have reminded the children once more of their **posture** and correctness in **pencil-holding** habits, have them **proceed** with the lesson according to the directions.

Further Helps for the Teacher

While the children are at the blackboard, it would be good if you would **use this opportunity to review some letters learned previously,** which the children do not use as frequently (for example, *x*). Do not take for granted that once a letter is learned, it is learned for good. The principle in relation to a motor skill such as handwriting is that **what is not repeated will be soon forgotten.**

Do not allow the children to make the numeral 5 begin with the across line. The children may think that it is easier that way, but it tends to round the top corner as speed is picked up, and this produces an illegible numeral.

Be sure that at the bottom of the forward-slanting line, the children start *up* with their curve. Going straight out from the bottom of the forward-slanting line produces an awkward looking numeral, while starting *up* with the curve, and making it larger and more complete, produces a numeral that is well balanced and more attractive.

See that **the forward-slanting line is slanted correctly.** Also be sure the points within the numeral are neatly and precisely made. **Watch to see that there is no gap or overlap at the junction of the forward-slanting line and the across line.**

Lesson 47
The Numeral 8

Lesson 47

The Numeral 8

99

Aim of the Lesson

To teach the numeral 8.

Directions

The children should trace over the strokes and numerals in row one. Row two is for practice. In row three they should trace over the numbers 58, 38, and 48 and use the remainder of the row to practice the numeral 8. Row four is a review of the numeral 5. The children should trace over it and copy it to the end of the row.

Conducting the Class

Ask the children these questions in relation to the picture:

"How many fingers do you have on your hands if you take your thumbs away?" (Eight.)

"Could you do very much with your hands without thumbs?" (Let the children try to pick up something without using their thumbs.)

Explain that God did not give us eight fingers by themselves, but He gave us two thumbs also to help us hold things more easily.

Tell the children, **"The numeral** 8 **is the numeral that you are** going to learn today. Let us look at it together. **How do you think it is made?"**

After they have given their ideas, **show them how by demonstrating.** As you demonstrate, **explain the formation of the numeral** as follows:

The numeral 8 **is begun just below the top line** toward the forward side of the numeral. From the starting point, **we curve back up to the top line, down,** and **around** to the middle line. **At the middle line we curve down. We curve about as far as we do for the letter** s, going down to the bottom line and back up a short distance. We **finish with a forward-slanting line** that touches **the starting point** and continues to the top line.

Send the children to the **blackboard** to **practice** this numeral. First of all, **have them trace around some figure** 8's several times. This exercise will help to give them the feel of the numeral. Do not be too concerned about accuracy in this exercise. In a second exercise, have them practice the numeral one stroke at a time; emphasize accuracy and proper form in making the numeral.

As the children complete their lesson, be on hand to correct any incorrect habits in either **posture, pencil holding,** or the **formation** of the numeral.

Further Helps for the Teacher

Be sure the children make the top and bottom parts of the 8 **the same size.** They may tend to make the bottom part larger than the top.

It may also be difficult for the children to make smooth curves on the *8* because of its tallness. Teach them to make the curves fairly rapidly, continuing to practice until their *8*'s are acceptable.

The numeral *8* should sit vertically on the bottom line. One should be able to draw a vertical line down each side and touch the points on each.

Lesson 48
Review of Curve-stroke Letters and Numerals.

Lesson 48   **Review of**

Curve-stroke Letters and Numerals

C   u

r   n   m

h   f

j   S

Aim for the Lesson

To thoroughly review the letters and numerals *c, u, r, n, m, h, f, j, s, 2, 3, 5, 8.*

Directions

In each row that begins with a letter or numeral, the children are to trace over each figure and copy it until the space allotted is filled. For the last few lines, the teacher can pick out the six letters or numerals that are most difficult for his students and have them practice them in those lines.

Conducting the Class

Explain to the children that they have now learned to write every small letter of the alphabet and all the numerals. But before they review the entire alphabet, **they are going to review the curve-stroke letters and numerals** that they have just learned.

Proceed in a similar manner as with previous reviews. If time permits, **have the children give you the stroke formation of each letter and numeral for this section.** At their desks or at the blackboard, **have them write down the answers to the following questions:**

"Which letters and numerals have curve lines?" (All of them.)

"Which letters or numerals have more than one curve?" (*m, s, 3, 8.*)

"Which letters or numerals have down lines?" (*u, r, n, m, h, f, j.*)

"Which letters or numerals in this lesson have across lines?" (*f, 2, 5.*)

"Which letters or numerals have lines that trace over each

143

other?" (*u, r, n, m, h, 3*—demonstrate what you mean, if necessary.)
    "Which letter or numeral goes below the line?" (*j.*)
    "Which letters or numerals are one space high?" (*u, r, n, m, s, e.*)
    "Which letters or numerals are two spaces high?" (*h, f, 2, 3, 5, 8.*)
    Following this drill, **have the children proceed with the lesson** according to the directions. Watch their work carefully as they do the lesson.

Further Helps for the Teacher

Be sure that your children are still meeting the goals outlined in Lessons 8, 14, 26, and 34.

In addition to these, **your children should have achieved the following goals in the last thirteen lessons** in relation to understanding and putting into practice the principles of letter formation for the thirteen letters and numerals they have just finished learning. These include—

1. the **ability to form a curve accurately** (their curves must not be too shallow, too deep, or too uneven);
2. the **ability to join curve lines with slanted, up, down, or across lines** easily, without producing an abrupt point at the junction;
3. the **ability to keep their curve lines separate from the straight lines;**
4. the **ability to retrace accurately;**
5. the **ability to keep the up and down lines** of letters such as *u, n, m,* and *h* **the right distance from each other,** not crowded too closely nor spread too far apart;
6. the **ability to begin a letter or numeral accurately when it does not begin on a line** (for example, *f*);
7. the **ability to make neat double curves,** such as in *s* and *8.*

For your quick reference, **here are the curve-stroke letters** with the strokes in the order in which they are composed:

    c—curve
    u—down, curve, up, down
    r—down, up, curve
    n—down, up, curve, down
    m—down, up, curve, down, up, curve, down
    h—down, up, curve, down

f—curve, down, across line
j—down, curve, dot
s—curve, curve
2—curve, f-s line, across line
3—curve, curve
5—f-s line, curve, across line
8—curve, curve, f-s line

Lesson 49
Review of the Alphabet (Part 1)

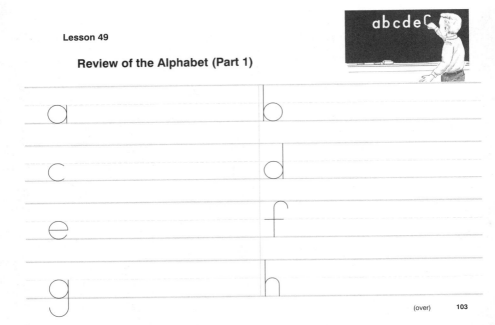

Lesson 49

Review of the Alphabet (Part 1)

(over)
103

Aim of the Lesson

To help the children establish the relationship between the letters they have learned by stroke groups and the same letters as they are found in alphabetical order; to review the first thirteen letters of the alphabet thoroughly and in an orderly manner.

Directions

The children should trace over each letter and copy it until the allotted space is full. In the last lines they are to copy the alphabet up to the letter *m* in order alphabetically.

146

Conducting the Class

Explain to the children at the beginning of the class period that since they have learned the small letters of the alphabet, they will need to remember how each letter was made. They will be using these letters more and more in time to come. Someday they will need to know the letters well enough that they can write them almost without thinking what strokes are used. But they will need a lot of practice in making the strokes and letters first.

Following the above discussion, **have your children come to the blackboard and draw several of each manuscript stroke** as you call out the names of the strokes.

At their desks, **have them look at the letters** that are printed on the two pages of the lesson **and give the correct strokes for each one,** in the proper order.

The children should then **proceed with the lesson,** filling out the rows as instructed. (See **"Further Helps for the Teacher"** for further suggestions.) Check to be sure they are **exercising good posture** and are **holding their pencils correctly.**

Further Helps for the Teacher

This would be a good opportunity to **look back over the goals of the review lessons** and to be sure that your children are meeting them. Check their alignment, letter straightness, and letter form, which includes their ability to make and join the manuscript strokes neatly and accurately. Check their curves and circles for evenness.

To rivet the necessity of correct letter form and to help ensure that the children do not become sloppy, have the children draw only two of each letter on each line. Then look over the letters they have drawn and **mark the letters that do not satisfy you. Have the children practice** these letters on other paper until you are satisfied. **Then have them complete each row.**

Lesson 50
Review of the Alphabet (Part 2)

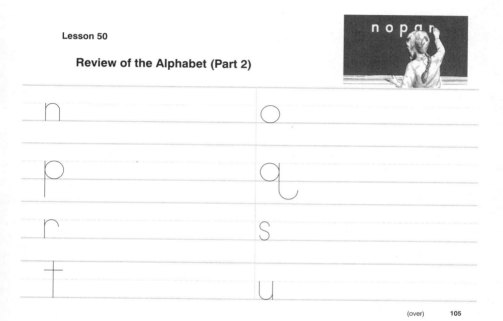

Lesson 50

Review of the Alphabet (Part 2)

n   o

p   q

r   s

t   u

(over)   105

Aim of the Lesson

To help the children establish the relationship between the letters they have learned by stroke groups and the same letters as they are found in alphabetical order; to review the last thirteen letters of the alphabet thoroughly and in an orderly manner.

Directions

The children should trace over each letter and copy it until the allotted space is full. In the last lines they should copy all thirteen letters in alphabetical order.

Conducting the Class

Introduce this lesson as a continuation of Lesson 49. **Explain to the children** that in the last lesson they reviewed the first thirteen letters of the alphabet and that today they are going to review the last thirteen letters.

Today would be a good day to **give the children extra practice and drill at the blackboard.** In the drill today, **have the children write letters on the blackboard, stroke by stroke,** as you call out numbers rhythmically. Work on just a few letters, possibly *w, a,* and *f,* in that order. Begin slowly and increase in speed. Do not continue the drill very long.

Following drill and practice of the letters under consideration, have the children go to their desks. Again, **have them match each letter with its stroke combination.** For a variation in doing this, **describe the strokes of certain letters and have them tell you what letter it is.** (Remember that *v, x,* and *y* have the same stroke combination.) Or associate each letter with a certain stroke combination and ask the children to tell you whether it is right or not, and if not, what is wrong with it.

Have the children **proceed with the lesson** according to the directions (refer to "Further Helps for the Teacher," paragraph 2), while you check to see that they are exercising good **posture** and **are holding their pencils correctly.**

Further Helps for the Teacher

Again, as in Lesson 49, check the **alignment, letter straightness,** and **letter form** of the children's letters.

Use the quality-checking method, which was introduced in the previous lesson. There it was suggested that you **have the children draw only two of each letter on each line before you check over their letters.** After you have checked their work, they can proceed to the end of the line, making improved letters with the corrections you have specified.

If you have **time, have the children print the entire alphabet** from beginning to end (on extra paper or the blackboard), so that they fully understand the sequence of the letters and can easily associate the handwriting alphabet with the reading alphabet with which they are familiar.

Lesson 51
Review of the Numerals

Lesson 51

Review of the Numerals

1   2   3
     4   5

1   2

3   4

5   6

7   8

(over)   107

Aim of the Lesson

To help the children establish the relationship between the numerals they have learned by stroke groups, and the same numerals as they are found in numerical order; to review the ten numerals thoroughly and in an orderly manner; to test the children on their understanding of the material covered in Unit 2.

Directions

The children should trace over each numeral and copy it until the allotted space is full. In the last several full lines, they should copy the entire alphabet and the ten numerals in order, as a test. (See the following for further instructions.)

Conducting the Class

Explain to the children **that** in today's lesson **they are going to review the ten numerals.**

Begin the class period by **sending the children to the blackboard.** If time permits, **have them print the entire alphabet** as a review for the test at the end of the lesson.

Next, **the children should print the numerals.** For variety in review, describe the stroke combination of the numeral, and then something the numeral describes that the children can count or already know. For example: "This numeral is made with one down line. This number of clocks is on the wall. What numeral is it?" Have them write the numeral on the board.

Following the numeral review, send the children back to their seats to **begin their lessons. Be sure that your children's numerals have accurate form and good quality;** that is, they should be made vertically with smooth lines, have proper height relationship, evenness of alignment on top and bottom (the strokes should come right to the line), and of course no lines should be misplaced, missing, added, or improperly joined.

In the last few lines, the children are to write the alphabet and numerals from memory, since this is a test of their understanding of the principles of letter formation.

Further Helps for the Teacher

Evaluate carefully the children's work in the last three rows. This test is to help you see how well the children have understood the formation of the small letters and numerals. You should be checking here also for accurate formation and good quality, watching the areas that were outlined above. **Grade on the basis of the thirty-six answers,** considering each unacceptable letter or numeral as one error.

It may seem to some teachers that there is not much need to teach the numerals in a penmanship course, since they learn them in arithmetic. However, the reason they should be taught here also is that in arithmetic, the main emphasis is on how to use the numerals in figuring, and the correct way of making the numerals is easily neglected. In penmanship, more time can be taken to learn how to form the numerals accurately, because this is the purpose of penmanship. If the teacher takes the time early in the child's school experience to teach the form of the numerals well, he can help keep his children from making mathematical errors because of inability to read their own writing, as well as save himself many paper-grading headaches.

Unit 3

Writing Words

Lessons 52–66

Introduction to Unit 3

In Unit 2 your children learned the manuscript letters and numerals. In Unit 3 they will be learning how to use these letters in the formation of words. The formation of words is a first step in making the learning of letters practical, and this should help to make the lessons interesting to your children.

The children no doubt are already familiar with how letters make up words, from reading, and have even done some writing of words. The purpose of this unit is to aid the children primarily in the proper spacing of letters within a word, and between the words themselves. It is also to establish in their minds the manner of word formation and to aid them in continued improvement of the small manuscript letters.

Each of the fifteen lessons in this unit will emphasize the use of one or usually two letters, in words. The majority of these words are taken from the first grade *Bible Nurture and Reader Series,* and the children (using this series) will already have learned most of them.

The letters will be taken alphabetically to lend variety and order to the learning process.

Now that your children have learned the complete alphabet, you should not allow them to write any letters any other way except that which they have learned in writing class. While previous to now you have had to make exception for those letters that had not yet been learned thoroughly, that is not now the case. So you should call the children's attention to any inaccuracy or carelessness in their writing, and be sure that they correct it. Of course, at this point, the capital letters will be excepted.

To help the children get the feel of proper spacing between letters in a word and between words in the pupil's book, you may have the children trace over each existing word previous to printing it, if you so desire.

In this unit you will want to be giving the children blackboard practice of one variety or another every day. As has been brought out

previously, blackboard drill is an important means of riveting principles and processes in a child's mind, as well as an aid to the teacher
in keeping up with a child's progress in learning.

Lesson 52
Using the Letters a and b in Words

Lesson 52

Using the Letters

a **and** b

in Words

and   are   at

be   obey   but   big

bad

5

Aim of the Lesson

To help the children understand how the letters *a* and *b* are placed when written in a word context; to teach how these letters are spaced in relation to other letters and words.

Directions

The words in the first, third, and fifth rows may be traced over if the teacher desires. The children are to copy one in row two, and row three in row four. In row five, the word *bad* should be copied two times, with the words correctly spaced.

Conducting the Class

Begin the class period by **discussing the new unit** with the children. Explain that, as they already know, letters are used to form words. But those **letters must be placed together correctly for each word to look right.** On the blackboard **show letters put together incorrectly** (either too far apart or too close together). Then **put several letters together in the correct way.** Your illustrations should show the children that if the letters forming words are not put together correctly, the words do not look right either.

Inform the children that in this lesson we are going to look at the **first two letters of the alphabet** and how they are spaced. **Draw each letter correctly spaced** within a word.

Explain to the children that as they make each letter, **they need to be sure** that the beginning of **each letter is just the right distance from the letter before it,** and that the space between each letter is the same distance. The **distance between the words must also be the same.**

Have the children go to the **blackboard** to **practice** some words themselves and then **complete their lesson** at their desks. Continue to keep an eye on their **posture, pencil holding,** and **paper placement.**

Further Helps for the Teacher

One **spacing problem** that sometimes occurs **with the letter** *a* should be demonstrated. **When the circle is begun, not enough room may be left for it to be completed well.** Using the word *bad,* show what happens when the circle of the *a* is begun too close to the letter *b*. Either it gets too close to the letter *b* (maybe even overlaps) or it gets squashed out of shape so that it will fit into the space.

Since any **letters with a backward-forming circle tend to be more difficult to space,** some children may have difficulty with the letter *d* also, as in the word *bad.* Help those children individually, explaining that in the next lesson they will learn more about spacing the letter *d*.

Right from the beginning of this unit, **the children should endeavor to space** *all* **their letters evenly,** not simply the letters they are studying just now. The reason for having each lesson deal with particular letters is to emphasize those letters along with any special problems the children may have with them.

Although spacing is especially emphasized in this unit, do not forget that **quality and accuracy** in letter formation **will continue to be important** and should not be neglected.

Letters should be spaced about one-fourth inch apart and **words three-fourths to one inch apart, for this size (one-inch) letters.**

Lesson 53
Using the Letters c and d in Words

Lesson 53

Using the Letters

c **and** d

in Words

cat can act

does read good

could

7

Aim of the Lesson

To help the children understand how the letters c and d are placed when written in a word context; to teach how these letters are spaced in relation to other letters or words.

Directions

If desired, the teacher first may have the children trace over the words in rows one, three, and five. Rows one and three should be copied in rows two and four. In row five the word *could* should be copied and properly spaced after the existing word.

Conducting the Class and Further Helps for the Teacher

In the beginning of this class period, **have the children come to the blackboard and practice the words they wrote in Lesson 52.** As the children do this, check to see whether they have really begun to learn how to space properly. Give them several words to print one right after another, to check on their word-spacing ability. Particularly check on the spacing of letters around the letters *a* and *b*.

Demonstrate the spacing of the letters *c* **and** *d* as they should be spaced within a word. **Explain and demonstrate also how some children may space these letters incorrectly.** Both letters present the problem discussed for *a* in the last lesson.

The letter *c* has a further problem because of the fact that it hardly appears to have right side. It is somewhat indefinite. **The tendency is** therefore **to make the letter following the letter** *c* **too close,** because the open space in the middle of the letter gives the impression of lots of room.

Have the children **practice several of the lesson words** at the blackboard as you supervise their spacing. At their desks they should **complete the lesson** according to the directions, again under your close supervision.

Lesson 54
Using the Letter e and f in Words

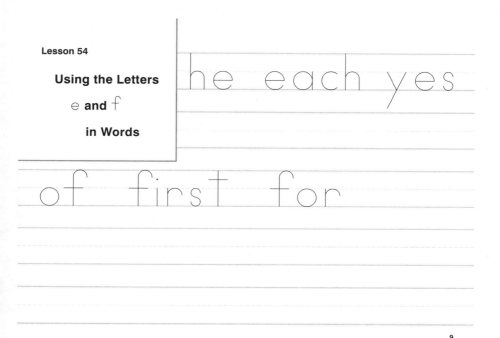

Lesson 54

Using the Letters

e **and** f

in Words

he each yes

of first for

9

Aim of the Lesson

To help the children understand how the letters *e* and *f* are placed when written in a word context; to teach how these letters are spaced in relation to other letters or words.

Directions

If desired, have the children trace over the words in rows one and three. They should then copy those words in rows two and four. This applies to the remainder of the lessons in this unit. In row three, the word *for* should also be copied in the space at the end of the line. The words *bad* and *could* should be called out or written on the board by the teacher for the children to copy in row five.

Conducting the Class

Begin the class period by **demonstrating on the blackboard the correct spacing of the letters** *e* **and** *f* in words. **Show them also how not to space** these letters (see "Further Helps for the Teacher"). **Give several illustrations** and ask the children, "Are these words [or letters] correctly spaced? If not, what's wrong?"

Have the children come to the blackboard and print several words from their lesson. **Help them with the spacing** of these words as well as with the general quality of their writing.

At their desks **have the children complete their lessons according to the directions. Do not forget** that you must tell the children what they are to print in row five.

Further Helps for the Teacher

Be sure you **do not neglect the quality of your children's writing in an interest in letter spacing.** Do not allow your children's letters to degenerate from the original teaching of those letters. Rather, they should improve.

Continue to insist upon good posture. To remind you what this consists of, it means: **sitting up straight, both feet on the floor,** and **both forearms on the desk.** One arm is to hold the paper, and the other is to do the writing.

The problem in this lesson is with the letter *f*. Because of the insignificant appearance of the across line, particularly its leftward extension, **it may be quite easy to place the letter** *f* **too close to the previous letter.**

Remember that it is the beginning of the across line, not the stem of the letter, that should be one-fourth inch from the previous letter.

Again, remember that you are not only looking for incorrect spacing in the letters *a* through *f*, but you should also correct spacing errors between any letters, particularly those that are not difficult to space.

Lesson 55
Using the Letters g and h in Words

Lesson 55

Using the Letters

g **and** h

in Words

good night

he she had help

light

11

Aim of the Lesson

To help the children understand how the letters *g* and *h* are placed when written in a word context; to teach how these letters are spaced in relation to other letters or words.

Directions

The words in rows one and three should be copied in rows two and four. In row five the word *light* should be copied twice, with special attention being given to spacing between each word.

Conducting the Class

Have the children **come to the blackboard to review the letters from Lesson 54** by practicing the words *yes* and *first*. They should first print *yes* and then *first*, and then reverse them for variety in spacing practice. Check particularly for **accurate word spacing.**

While the children are at the blackboard, **briefly discuss the new lesson's letters** and have the children **practice several words from the lesson.** The letters *g* and *h* are not more difficult to space than any previous letters and should not require any special instruction.

The children should complete the lesson according to the directions.

Further Helps for the Teacher

If you have time, **give a drill** on the letter forms of the letters *a* through *h*. One drill you might want to use could be called an **add-to drill. Name a letter** and then have the children print the letter stroke by stroke. **Each child should call out the next stroke in his turn and then place it on the letter.** For example, with the letter *a*, John would say, "Circle," and then place it on the board. Then Mary would say, "Down line," and place it on the board. Continue making letters in this way to produce words, such as *bad, bed, head,* and *had.*

If any child has much of a problem with **incorrect letter spacing,** you can **draw short lines horizontally between the letters.** This will show him just how far off his spacing is.

Since first grade children will likely have difficulty fathoming three-fourths of an inch, or even one inch, explain to them that **the space between words is about the width of the letter** *w*. When writing, they should try to imagine a letter *w* in that space and fit their words around that imaginary letter. (For the present, this means the small letter *w*; after they learn capitals, they will think of capital *W*'s. See Lesson 103.)

Lesson 56
Using the Letters i and j in Words

Lesson 56

Using the Letters

i **and** j

in Words

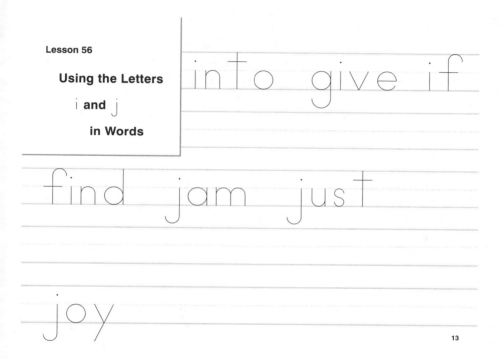

Aim of the Lesson

To help the children understand how the letters *i* and *j* are placed when written in a word context; to teach how these letters are spaced in relation to other letters or words.

Directions

The words in rows one and three should be copied in rows two and four. In row five the word *joy* should be copied twice, paying special attention to spacing between each word.

Conducting the Class

Draw the letters *i* **and** *j* on the blackboard. Ask the children to tell you **what about these two letters make them different** from most other letters of the alphabet. They will likely first mention that **both letters are dotted,** which is correct. But you should draw their attention to the fact that the letter *i* is one down line and so is the upper part of the letter *j*. A down line by itself will not take up as much space as a letter such as *a*. **Compare the two letters** *i* **and** *j* **with the letter** *a* **to show the relative differences in width.** By **using the word** *give*, **demonstrate** on the blackboard how little space the letter *i* takes up in a word. Show the children that they should still leave the same amount of space on each side of *i* and *j* as they do for the other letters.

Have the children come to the **blackboard** and **practice** on the words *give, into,* and *jam*. They should print them in order with proper spacing between each word.

At their seats, the children should **proceed with the lesson** according to the directions. Be sure to supervise their work and **check each area** well: quality, form, spacing, posture, pencil holding, and paper placement.

Further Helps for the Teacher

Remind the children **not to forget to dot the letters** i and *j* and to **make their dots large enough to be seen. Be sure that the stems** of the *i* and *j* **remain** vertical, and that the **down line and curve** of the letter *j* **blend properly.** Also remind them to allow extra space for the curve of the *j* when they begin the letter.

If you have time, **do a counting drill on the letter** *i*. This should be a relatively easy letter for the children to drill, because it has a simple one-two count. Begin slowly, picking up speed gradually. Do not go too fast, or continue the drill too long, to prevent frustration.

Lesson 57
Using the Letters k and l in Words

Lesson 57

Using the Letters

k **and** l

in Words

make kind

like all little help

glad

15

Aim of the Lesson

To help the children understand how the letters *k* and *l* are placed when written in a word context; to teach how these letters are spaced in relation to other letters or words.

Directions

The words in rows one and three should be copied in rows two and four. In row five, the emphasis is on proper word spacing. The word *glad* should be copied twice.

169

Conducting the Class

At the beginning of the class period, **have the children review** on the blackboard **the spacing of the letters** i **and** j from the previous lesson. They can do this by practicing the words *into* and *jam* four times in the following sequence: *into, jam, jam, into.* Be sure both word and letter spacing are accurate and consistent.

After the children are back at their seats, **print the letters** k **and** l on the blackboard. **Discuss the difference** between the two letters, pointing out that the letter l is the same width as the letter i from the previous lesson, while k is the same width as the letter a and similar letters. Therefore, **the letter** l **will not** look as though it were **taking up as much space as the letter** k. However, the same amount of space will be between both k and l and the letters around them.

Return the children to the **blackboard** to **practice** the letters for today's lesson. Have them use the words *make* and *little* in doing so.

At their seats, the children should **complete the lesson** according to the directions above.

Further Helps for the Teacher

The letter k is one of the more difficult letters because of its somewhat **complex arrangement of lines.** Check your children's work in the formation of this letter to see that they remember how it is to be made. If necessary, **remind them where and how the lines are joined together.**

As an incidental point, draw the children's attention to the fact that the **letter** k **is actually started like the letter** l. Those two letters have not previously been directly associated. Each time you can make a new association, you are helping to more firmly establish the letter forms in the children's minds.

Even though the children have not practiced spacing **the letter** t (as in *little*), they should be sure to **place them far enough apart** that they can cross them without danger of overlapping the crosses. You may not need to say anything to them at this time. As the children copy the word, they will likely copy the proper spacing too.

Lesson 58
Using the Letter m in Words

Lesson 58

Using the

Letter m

in Words

made some

man animal me

him

17

Aim of the Lesson

To help the children understand how the letter *m* is placed when written in a word context; to teach how this letter is spaced in relation to other letters or words.

Directions

The words in rows one and three should be copied in rows two and four. In row five, the word *him* should be copied two times, with proper spacing between each word.

Conducting the Class

Have the children look at the letter *m,* which you have placed on the blackboard. **Discuss the width of the letter** *m.* This is one thing that sets this letter apart and is also related to spacing within the letter. Only **one letter in the alphabet is wider** than the letter *m,* and that is the letter *w.*

Explain to the children that **they should not try to squash the letter** *m* to make it fit into a space as small as other letters. **But neither should they spread it out too far. Demonstrate by using examples,** one above the other, of a crowded *m* in a word, a spread-out *m* in a word, and a correctly written *m* in a word.

The children should **drill at the blackboard** on the words *made* and *him* from today's lesson, and the words *like* and *help* from the previous lesson for review. See "Further Helps for the Teacher" for extra drill.

At their seats, the children should **proceed with their lessons** according to the directions, while maintaining **proper posture** and **holding their pencils correctly.**

Further Helps for the Teacher

For further drill with the letter *m,* if you have extra time, **have the children make rows of** *m***-humps.** They should begin making a regular *m,* but just keep adding humps to the end of the row. While making these humps, the children should also be maintaining straight stems, proper distance between stems, and properly rounded humps. This exercise is to help the children get the feel of making the letter *m.*

Learning handwriting is an adding-to process. **As soon as something has been learned, it must be added to the list of that which must be continually reviewed,** so that it does not with carelessness or poor memory slip away. So we would like to remind you again not to give all your attention in this unit to spacing. You must not neglect the form and quality of the letters, even though spacing is the main theme. Admittedly, keeping up mentally with several different areas of penmanship at one time is difficult, but failure to do so will be almost certain to guarantee failure in your teaching of penmanship.

Lesson 59
Using the Letters n and o in Words

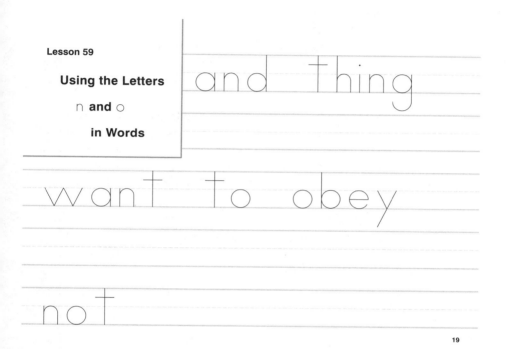

Aim of the Lesson

To help the children understand how the letters *n* and *o* are placed when written in a word context; to teach how these letters are spaced in relation to other letters or words.

Directions

The words in rows one and three should be copied in rows two and four. In row five, the word *not* should be copied twice, with accurate word and letter spacing.

Conducting the Class

Ask someone to read the words in the second line out loud to the class. Then **ask them these questions:**

"Who should want to obey?" (*We* should want to obey.)

"Whom should *we* want to obey?" (We should want to obey our parents, teachers, ministers, and God.)

Have the children go to the **blackboard** and **review** the letter from the previous lesson, **practicing the words** *animal* **and** *man.* They should print these words twice in one row, reversing them the second time as described in Lesson 57 ("Conducting the Class," first paragraph).

Give the children a **brief introduction to the two letters.** Since there is not much special instruction to be given in relation to the spacing of the letters *n* and *o*, the children can probably go ahead and **practice words using those letters** without a prior demonstration. While they are at the **blackboard,** have them **practice the words** *and* **and** *not.*

Following blackboard practice, the children should go back to their seats and **proceed to complete the lesson.**

Further Helps for the Teacher

How is the children's **circle formation** in this lesson? Are they able to draw a circle accurately and smoothly?

Lesson 60
Using the Letters p and q in Words

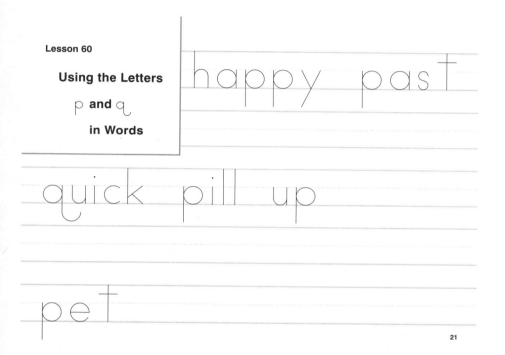

Lesson 60

Using the Letters

p **and** q

in Words

Aim of the Lesson

To help the children understand how the letters *p* and *q* are placed when written in a word context; to teach how these letters are spaced in relation to other letters or words.

Directions

The words in rows one and three should be copied in rows two and four. In row five, the word *pet* should be copied twice, with accurate word and letter spacing.

Conducting the Class

Begin the class period by **reviewing the form of the letters** p **and** q. **Have the children tell you how these letters are made,** asking several students to make the strokes for the letters on the blackboard. This will add variety in approach, as well as draw the children's minds directly to the formation of the letters.

Using the words *happy* and *quick*, **demonstrate the spacing of** p **and** q within those words. Show the children that they are to **space the letter** q **from the top of the letter,** not from the tail. (This is the only letter that has this exception.)

The children should **practice** *happy* **and** *quick* **on the blackboard** and also the words *thing* and *not* from the previous lesson.

At their desks, they should, under your supervision, **complete their lesson** according to the directions.

Further Helps for the Teacher

The children should be able to see that there are **similarities between the letters** p **and** q. Both letters are based on the circle and the down line. Both letters have parts that go below the line. A q looks like a backward p with the addition of a curve at the bottom.

Check the manner in which your children are writing their names. Are you insisting that their names be written just as well as the rest of their writing? (The children's names will be written somewhat smaller than their writing in the penmanship lessons, so you may not find height, proportion, and so forth quite as exact. You must be the judge of what is an acceptable standard in this.) How are they making the capital letters which begin their names? Are they learning an incorrect form, which will hinder their learning the letter correctly later?

Lesson 61
Using the Letter r in Words

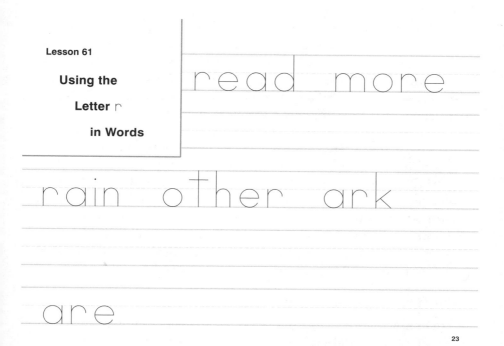

Lesson 61

Using the

Letter ⌐

in Words

read more

rain other ark

are

23

Aim of the Lesson

To help the children understand how the letter *r* is placed when written in a word context; to teach how this letter is spaced in relation to other letters or words.

Directions

The words in rows one and three should be copied in rows two and four. In row five, the word *are* should be copied twice, with accurate word and letter spacing.

Conducting the Class

Place the letter *r* on the blackboard. Draw the children's attention to its formation by **asking them to tell you what letter could be made by adding a down line to the end of the letter.** (The letter *n*.) You could also very **quickly review the stroke formation** of the letter *r* with the children.

Demonstrate the spacing of the letter *r* by using the word *more*. Print the word carefully and accurately on the blackboard. Then ask the children to tell you whether your letter *r* is spaced right. Likely they will think there is too much space on the forward side of the letter, between *r* and *e*. Show them that the space on each side is really the same. It *looks* as if there were more space on that side, but that is because we must space from the end of the curve rather than from the stem of the letter. Show what would happen if the next letter were spaced from the stem rather than from the curve.

Have the children come to the **blackboard** and **practice the words** *rain* **and** *ark*. They may need to print the words several times until you are satisfied with their spacing. Also they should **review the previous lesson by drill on the words** *pill* **and** *up*.

At their desks the children should **complete the written lesson** according to the directions, under your supervision.

Further Helps for the Teacher

Do not neglect any spacing inaccuracies that may appear in the letters the children have already practiced for spacing, particularly letters such as *a, d, i,* and *j*, which often cause spacing problems. You must look for and correct these errors in order to adequately reinforce what you have taught.

Remember to check each day on the children's letter formation, especially in relation to the letter(s) under consideration. Also remember to gently **correct any faulty posture or pencil holding.** Be sure the children are sitting straight with both feet on the floor, both arms on the desk, and pencils held loosely, not pinched.

Lesson 62
Using the Letter s in Words

Lesson 62

Using the

Letter s

in Words

cars   sore

lives   has   sad

son

25

Aim of the Lesson

To help the children understand how the letter *s* is placed when written in a word context; to teach how this letter is spaced in relation to other letters or words.

Directions

The words in rows one and three should be copied in rows two and four. In row five, the word *son* should be copied twice, with accurate word and letter spacing.

Conducting the Class

At the beginning of this class period, the children should be given a **drill on the letters** *i* **through** *r* at the blackboard. Each letter should be printed twice, and they should be properly spaced from each other in rows across the board. The children should also **print the word** *are* **twice** in a row with proper spacing.

Demonstrate the letter *s* **and how it is spaced** by using the words *has* and *sad*. The children will need to be careful in spacing this letter, because it, like the letter *a*, **begins at the side away from the previous letter. This will tend to leave a space that is too small on the left side of the letter.**

At the board, the children should **make a short row of** *s*'**s,** properly spaced, and then **practice the letter in the words** *has* **and** *sad*. At their seats they should **proceed with their lesson** according to the directions.

Further Helps for the Teacher

Notice again that **this letter** contains no straight lines or full circles. It **can** therefore **be considered an indefinite letter.** The children may tend to make it tilted to one side or the other, too wide, too narrow, or with unevenly arranged curves. **So you may need to reteach to some children the formation of the letter** along with its spacing.

Lesson 63
Using the Letter t in Words

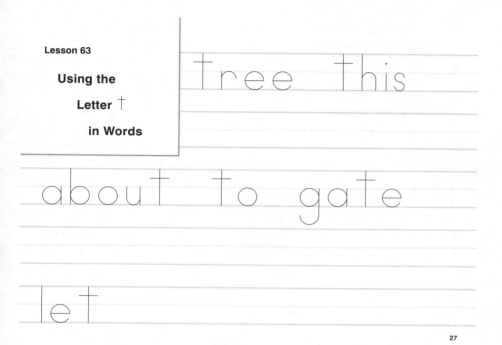

Lesson 63

Using the

Letter †

in Words

tree this

about to gate

let

27

Aim of the Lesson

To help the children understand how the letter *t* is placed when written in a word context; to teach how this letter is spaced in relation to other letters or words.

Directions

The words in rows one and three should be copied in rows two and four. In row five, the word *let* should be copied twice, with accurate word and letter spacing.

181

Conducting the Class

At the blackboard, the children should **review the spacing of the letter** *s* by practicing the words *has* and *sad.* They should print each word twice, reversing them the second time, as outlined in a previous lesson.

After the children are back at their seats, **demonstrate the letter** *t*, **showing how it is to be spaced.** Do so by using the word *gate.* Although the children have already been spacing the letter *t*, they have not received much specific instruction in relation to it. Primarily **the children need to understand that the letter is to be spaced from the ends of the across line.** Show them that they will need to draw the down line far enough from the letter just before to allow plenty of room for the across line. You can show why with the word *salt.* Draw the down line close to the letter *l* and then cross it. If the down line is brought that close, the cross will need to be made very short or it will cross the *l* also. The children must be careful to leave enough space so that this does not happen.

At the blackboard the children should print the words *gate* **and** *about,* with **proper spacing.** At their desks they **should proceed with their lesson** according to the directions, as you supervise their work and correct any improper habits of writing, **posture,** or **pencil holding.**

Further Helps for the Teacher

Pay **special attention to the children's across lines** for the letter *t*. Are their crosses at the proper distance between the top and middle line? Are they evenly spaced on each side?

For children of first grade level, remember that **they will learn more from your corrections** while they are doing their work **than from the class explanations and demonstrations.** While these are necessary, do not depend on them to do the whole job. Be there while the children are working to help them with form and spacing.

Lesson 64
Using the Letters u and v in Words

Lesson 64

Using the Letters

u and v

in Words

us fuss up

very raven

but

29

Aim of the Lesson

To help the children understand how the letters *u* and *v* are placed when written in a word context; to teach how these letters are spaced in relation to other letters or words.

Directions

The words in rows one and three should be copied in rows two and four. In row five, the word *but* should be copied twice, with accurate word and letter spacing.

Conducting the Class

Demonstrate the letters *u* **and** *v* by using the words *fuss* and *raven*. **Spacing these two letters** will not be extraordinarily difficult, so use your time to emphasize a review of the form of the letters.

Remind the children as you demonstrate that the **top parts of the letter** *u* **are straight lines,** not curved. The stems on their *u*'s should not be squeezed together or spread apart too far. With the letter *v*, remind them that **the lines** making up the letter **should be slanted "just right."** The two top points should be the right distance apart from each other. **Demonstrate the incorrect extremes of slant** so the children know what to avoid. With both *u* and *v*, remind them to **be sure to make their letters touch the lines** they should touch at the top and bottom of the letter.

As the children come to the **blackboard** and **practice** the words *fuss* and *raven*, check their work for form and spacing inaccuracies. Have them also **review the last lesson by printing the word** *let* twice on the blackboard.

At their desk they should **proceed with the lesson** according to the directions, as you again check their work.

Further Helps for the Teacher

Check the children's writing for unevenness, in relation both to their curved lines and their straight lines. They will improve in this area if you are careful to help them do so.

For extra drill, call your children's attention to **the very first lesson** in their book. **Have them again try to draw a neat house** with straight walls as they did in that lesson. They will enjoy the variety, and it will help them in their formation of straight lines.

Lesson 65
Using the Letters w and x in Words

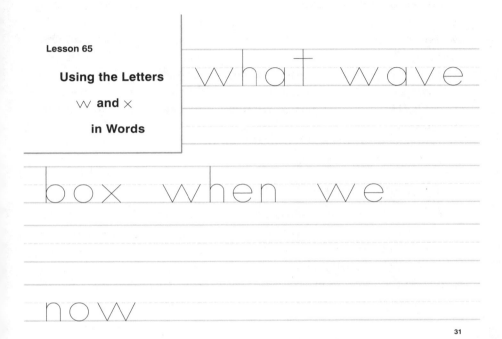

31

Aim of the Lesson

To help the children understand how the letters *w* and *x* are placed when written in a word context; to teach how these letters are spaced in relation to other letters or words.

Directions

The words in rows one and three should be copied in rows two and four. In row five, the word *now* should be copied twice, with accurate word and letter spacing.

Conducting the Class

Draw the two letters *w* **and** *x* **on the board.** Begin the class by **asking the children to tell you their stroke combinations.** Discuss the fact that **slanting lines make up both letters.**

Demonstrate the spacing of the letters *w* **and** *x* by using the words *what* and *box*. Explain to the children that **the letter** *w* **is a very wide letter.** It is the widest letter in the alphabet, even a little wider than the letter *m*. **The letter** *x* **is the same width as the average letter** and is spaced like any other letter. **With both letters,** it is important to **slant the lines accurately.**

At the **blackboard** the children should **practice** the words *wave* and *box*. They should **review the previous lesson by printing the words** *us* and *very* twice, reversing them the second time.

At their desks, the children should **proceed with their lesson** according to the directions.

Further Helps for the Teacher

It would be good in this lesson to **review the manuscript strokes** again with the children. **Draw the strokes on the blackboard, and ask the children to name the strokes.** Or have them draw the strokes at the board as you call them out. It is important to review the basics of writing fairly frequently, so that the children keep well acquainted with the foundation of their writing.

Lesson 66
Using the Letters y and z in Words

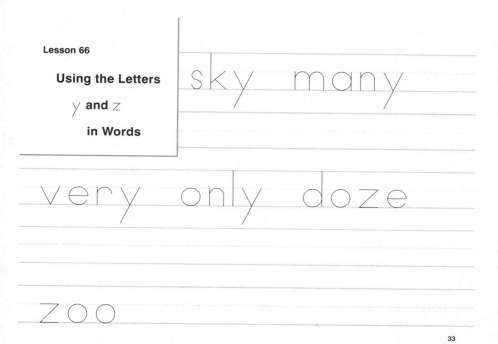

Lesson 66

Using the Letters

y **and** z

in Words

sky many

very only doze

zoo

33

Aim of the Lesson

To help the children understand how the letters *y* and *z* are placed when written in a word context; to teach how these letters are spaced in relation to other letters or words.

Directions

The words in rows one and three should be copied in rows two and four. In row five, the word *zoo* should be copied twice, with accurate word and letter spacing.

Conducting the Class

Demonstrate the spacing of the letters y **and** z by using the words *sky* and *doze*. **Have the children tell you the stroke combinations** of these two letters.

Some children may find it difficult to always space the letter y **correctly.** Because only one small point sticks out on each side of the letter, it may be easy to bring other letters too close without appearing crowded. Help the children space letters around the letter y from the top of the letter, not from where the letter crosses the bottom line.

The letter z **should be no problem in spacing** unless the children are having problems with other letters also.

Have the children go to the **blackboard** and **practice the words** *sky* **and** *doze*. Following this they should **review the letters** s **through** z by printing the following words on the blackboard: *has, tree, fuss, raven, wave, box, very,* and *zoo.* Check each word for proper letter spacing.

At their desks, the children should **proceed with the lesson** according to the directions.

Further Helps for the Teacher

If you have time, or **see a need for more practice** for your children, **have them use the backs of their lesson pages** to practice words with letters that have caused them trouble, either in spacing or in formation. This can be done on an individual level or on a class level, whichever you desire.

Although your children have now finished this unit in which much attention has been given to spacing, this does not mean that their problems with spacing will all be solved from here on. **You will now need to add spacing to the list of items for which you will need to check the children's work.** In the next unit, you will be teaching another type of spacing. Teaching capital letters will require that the children learn to space between capital and small letters and eventually between capital letters.

Unit 4

Forming
Capital Letters

Lessons 67–102

Introduction to Unit 4

You as an adult will not need to think for long to recall a number of uses for capital letters. Here are a few you may think of: at the beginning of a sentence, for emphasis, and for names of the Godhead, people, cities, roads, buildings, rivers, mountains, oceans, pets, months, and days of the week.

Your children have already been introduced to the capital letter in reading. The list of capital letters is in the front of this book. They have probably looked over them and maybe even experimented a little with writing them. You have taught them at least the one capital letter necessary to write their first names. But now they are going to be learning the capital letters more thoroughly, much in the same manner that they learned the small letters.

The lessons in this section will be introduced similarly to the lessons in Unit 2. The arrangement of letters will be somewhat different, since the letters are formed differently and we want to be able to build the stroke formation of each letter on previous letters. There will be four sections in this unit just as there were in Unit 2, each dealing with letters using different types of strokes.

Although you will be concentrating on capital letters, the children will still be using small letters far more than capital letters in their work during this time. Therefore, do not fail to remind the children of proper formation of the small letters and proper spacing. Remember that at this point in the child's learning experience, it only takes a short period of neglect on your part for your children to develop bad habits in writing. Maintaining constant vigilance is the most important thing to remember to keep your children's writing on track.

Lesson 67
Capital Letter L

Lesson 67

Capital Letter L

Lord

life

37

Aim of the Lesson

To teach the formation of the capital *L*.

Directions

The children should trace over the strokes and letters in row one. Row two is for practice of the letter *L*. In row three and the beginning of row four, the children are to copy the word *Lord* at least twice, once in row three and once in row four. The word *life* is to be copied once in the space following it.

Conducting the Class

Introduce the writing of capital letters to the children. Review with the children **what they already know** about capital letters. They likely have already studied capital letters in other subjects and know some of their uses, such as that they always begin names of people and places. **Tell them that now they are going to be learning all the capital letters** very much in the same way that they have already learned the small letters: **by the strokes which make them up.**

Explain that **first they are going to learn to make the capital letters that have down and across lines.** The **first** of these on our list is **the letter L.**

Draw the letter L on the blackboard. Have one of the children come to the board and **place beside the capital** L **a small** l. This is to aid the children in associating the two forms of L more firmly.

Explain the formation of the letter L. **By asking questions,** get the children to tell you how the letter is made. The letter is made with **two lines:** a **down line** followed by an **across line.** Emphasize to the children that the manuscript letter L, as **all manuscript capital letters, fits exactly in the space between the bottom and the top line.** There are no short capital letters, or below-the-line capital letters. Also emphasize that the letter L is made without lifting the pencil between strokes.

Have the children go to the blackboard and draw the letter several times. Upon returning to their seats, they should receive their lesson instructions and **proceed with the lesson** accordingly. Make your rounds from one child to another, checking for accuracy as they do their work.

Further Helps for the Teacher

Be sure the children have associated well the capital letter L with the small letter l. **In most of the lessons** in this unit **there will be a word which contains the small counterpart of the capital letter learned.** Draw the children's attention to this in each lesson. In this lesson, it is the word *life.*

Many times the down line of the letter L is made slanted one way or the other, usually to the right. Be sure your children are not among those who do so.

Again, watch their **word and letter spacing** in the two words they are to copy, and—do not neglect good **posture and pencil-holding** habits.

Lesson 68
Capital Letter F

Lesson 68

Capital Letter F

Fred

fire

39

Aim of the Lesson

To teach the formation of the capital letter *F*.

Directions

The children should trace over the strokes and letters in row one. In row two they should practice the letter *F* on their own. In row three and the beginning of row four, they should print the word *Fred* twice, once in each row. In row four the word *fire* should be copied once.

Conducting the Class

Begin the class period by drawing the letters *L* and *F* on the blackboard. Ask the children to show you one thing that is the same about the two letters. (Both letters have a two-space down line.) None of the other lines are the same.

Move right into the **demonstration and explanation** of the formation **of the letter** *F*. **Bring the difference between the letters** *L* **and** *F* into your explanation. In the letter *L*, the across line is at the bottom of the letter, whereas the letter *F* has two across lines, one at the top and one in the middle. Next, explain the order of strokes for the letter *F*. **The first stroke is** the same as that of the letter *L*. It is **the down line. The next stroke is the across line at the top.** This line starts at the down line and goes out the same distance as the bottom line of *L*. **The third stoke is the line in the middle.** It starts at the down line and also goes across, but not quite as far out as the top line.

Following this explanation, **place a small letter** *f* **near the capital** *F* for comparison, and tell the children that we want to see how the two are different. Show them that even though they look somewhat alike, they are made in different ways.

Following a short period of **board practice,** have the children **proceed with their lesson** according to the directions.

Further Helps for the Teacher

Be sure your children do not begin using capital letters in place of small letters, or vice versa. Teach them to keep each one in its proper place.

Always **be sure** when teaching or reviewing any letter with up or down lines that **the lines are being made straight, not slanted.**

Give a **spot check on the way papers are being placed** on the children's desks. They should be very nearly straight up and down for right-handers, slanted to the right for left-handers.

Lesson 69
Capital Letter E

Lesson 69

Capital Letter E

Eve

41

Aim of the Lesson

To teach the formation of the capital letter *E*.

Directions

The children should trace over the strokes and letters in row one. In row two they should practice the letter *E*. In rows three and four, they should first trace over the word *Eve* and then copy it five times.

Conducting the Class

Begin the class period by having a short **board review of the letters L and F and the manuscript strokes,** along with any other letter that you feel is causing the children a problem.

Have the children return to their seats. **Ask this question,** "Who knows what letter will be made if we put the capital letter L and the capital letter F together one on top of the other?" (The letter E, which is the letter we are studying today.) **Show what happens by first drawing the letter L and then placing the letter F on top of it.**

Explain to the children, "Although a capital E can be made by making an L and putting an F *on top of it,* **that is not the best way to make it.** Who can think of a way that would be better and would want to show us on the blackboard?" Likely the children will be able to think of the best way before too long. Ask questions in relation to the kind (down, across) and number (four) of strokes that make up the letter and then go on to give the **order of strokes for the letter.** They are: **down line, first; top across line, second; middle across line, third;** and **bottom across line, fourth.** Show the children that the top and bottom strokes are just as long as they were on the letters L and F and that the middle stroke is the same length as the middle stroke of the letter F.

Give the instructions for **proceeding with the lesson.** Be sure to call the children's attention to how much difference there is between the capital letter E and the small letter e. Capital E is somewhat box-shaped, and small e is more like a circle.

Further Helps for the Teacher

Be sure the children do not make the letter E as an F-L combination. They should make it in the proper way. The F-L combination is to be given as a memory aid to help the form of the letter stick in their minds.

In the last two lines, check for **correct word and letter spacing.**

Although you cannot expect your children to get their **across lines** exactly perfect in length, you should **be sure that they are at least reasonably correct. The middle line should in each case be noticeably shorter** than the top and bottom lines, which should be nearly equal in length.

While the children are doing lines three and four, it would be good to ask them what they remember about the character of Eve.

Lesson 70
Capital Letter I

Lesson 70

Capital Letter I

Ida

ice

43

Aim of the Lesson

To teach the formation of the capital letter *I*.

Directions

The children should trace over the strokes and letters in row one. In row two, the children should copy the capital letter *I*. In rows three and four, the words *Ida* and *ice* should be traced over once and copied twice.

Conducting the Class

With the children at their seats, **print the capital letter _I_ on the blackboard with the small letter** _i_ beside it. Have the children **compare** the two letters and tell you how the capital letter is different from the small letter. (The capital letter has no dot, is two spaces tall, and has a short line across the top and the bottom.)

Demonstrate and explain the order of strokes on the blackboard. **The first stroke is a down line** from the top line to the bottom line. **Next is the across stroke at the top,** which begins on the back side of the down line, goes forward touching the very top of the down line, and goes a short distance on the other side. **The bottom across stroke is just like the top stroke.**

Have the children practice the letter _I_ a few times. Then give them instructions for the lesson and have them **proceed** according to the directions.

Further Helps for the Teacher

Be sure that the children understand that **the across lines are to begin** _before_ **the down line, not right at it** as with the letter _E_. Also help the children get their **across strokes evenly centered on the down line,** and not too long.

Lesson 71
Capital Letter T

Lesson 71

Capital Letter T

Tim

Time

45

Aim of the Lesson

To teach the formation of the capital letter *T.*

Directions

The children should trace over the strokes and letters in row one. Row two is for their practice of the letter. In rows three and four, they should trace over each word and copy it twice.

Conducting the Class

At the beginning of the class period, **compare the capital letter _T_ with the capital letter _I_**. The two letters are made similarly. In comparing, show the children these things: that the letter _T_ has a down line like the letter _I_, that it does _not_ have a line across the bottom as does the letter _I_, that the line across the top of the letter _T_ is about twice as long as the line across the top of the letter _I_.

The letter _T_ is made up of only two strokes, a down line and an **across line.** The down line is made first, going from the top line to the bottom line. The across line is then drawn across the top, from left to right.

Have the children go to the **blackboard** and **practice** the letter as you watch, correct, and check their accuracy. To help them with spacing, have them print the word _Tim_ several times.

At their seats, the children should be **given their instructions for the lesson.** Be sure they are **sitting up straight** and **holding their pencils correctly** before they begin.

Further Helps for the Teacher

As you will notice, that capital _T_ in the word _Tim_ appears to be quite a distance from the rest of the word at the first glance. The reason, of course, for this distance is to maintain consistent spacing. This will be more apparent if you **space with your eyes from the end of the across stroke rather than from the down stroke.** Explain to the children that the letter is to be spaced just like between small letters. If at some time or other the child spaces a short letter from the downstroke rather than from the end of the across stroke, this should not be considered too serious at this point.

Also, **do not be too exacting in the length of the cross stroke.** Without using a ruler, it is just about impossible to draw that long a line with perfectly correct length. However, **be sure that it is not as short as the line across the top of** _I_. The children are more likely to get it too short than too long.

In teaching straight-line letters, **work on keeping the lines as waver free as possible.** This goal will not be accomplished immediately with first grade students, but work hard on it. Your children will draw straighter, more waver-free lines as they grow more sure of themselves. This will happen through age, practice, and teacher-coached effort.

Lesson 72
Capital Letter H

Lesson 72

Capital Letter H

Helen

her

47

Aim of the Lesson

To teach the formation of the capital letter *H*.

Directions

In row one, the children should trace over the strokes and letters. Row two is for practice of the letter *H*. In rows three and four, the word *Helen* should be traced over and copied at least twice. The word *her* should be traced over and copied once.

202

Conducting the Class

On the blackboard, **introduce the letter** *H* to the children. Ask them to tell you any *names* they can think of that begin with the *H* sound.

Place the small letter *h* **beside the capital letter** for comparison.

Ask the children to give you the strokes for the letter *H*. Although they should be able to do this readily, **they may not be able to tell you the correct order** of the strokes. Therefore, be sure to get across that **the two down lines are made first,** before **the across line is made.**

Send the children to the **blackboard** to **practice** the letter a number of times. The first time they draw the letter, **have them draw it together with you.** Have them name each stroke as they make it.

At their seats, they should **proceed with the lesson** according to the directions.

Further Helps for the Teacher

With the letter *H* it is quite **important that the down lines be made correctly.** One important area to watch is to be sure the lines are made without slant. This will very definitely affect the appearance of the letter.

One error children often make with this letter is to make the down lines an incorrect distance apart. **Generally the lines are made too close together.** The children should be taught to make the lines just far enough apart that the across line can be as long as the space between the bottom line and the middle line (about one-half inch for one-inch-high writing). Demonstrate this.

While the children are practicing the letter at the blackboard is a good time to help them make the down lines right.

Lesson 73
Review of Straight-line Capitals

Lesson 73

Review of

Straight-line

Capitals

49

Aim of the Lesson

To review the formation of the capital letters *L, F, E, I, T,* and *H.*

Directions

The children should trace over the capital letter at the beginning of each row. They should then fill out the space provided with copies of each letter.

Conducting the Class

As a means of review at the beginning of the class period, **have the children go to the blackboard and write each of the capital letters** learned in the previous six lessons. They should do this until you are satisfied that they are making them correctly. For purposes of association, **they should also write the lower-case (small) form of each letter** beside each capital form.

At their seats, **ask them to tell you the strokes and order of strokes** composing each letter in this section. **Following are the stroke combinations** for the six capital letters under consideration:

L—down, across
F—down, across, across
E—down, across, across, across
I—down, across, across
T—down, across
H—down, down, across

Have the children **proceed to do the lesson** according to the directions. Before they begin, be sure they are maintaining **correct posture** and are **holding their pencils correctly.**

Further Helps for the Teacher

Glance back over the goals established in the review lessons for small letters (see especially Lesson 48). Are your children still able to meet the goals outlined in those lessons?

Following are goals the children should meet in this lesson:

1. **They should be able to form accurately and neatly the six letters** reviewed in this lesson. This includes making down lines that do not slant one direction or the other and cross lines that are a satisfactory length for the various letters.

2. **They should be able to space all the small letters** fairly accurately, as well as the six letters learned in the last six lessons.

Lesson 74
Capital Letter X

Lesson 74

Capital Letter ✕

Aim of the Lesson

To teach the formation of the capital letter *X*.

Directions

The children should trace over the strokes and letters in row one. Row two is for their practice of the letter *X*. In row three, the children should trace over and copy the word *Xenia* and then trace over the letter *L* and copy it to the end of the row. In row four, the word *extra* should be traced over and copied and then the numeral *4* traced over and copied to the end of the row.

Conducting the Class

Begin the class period by telling the children that they are now going to begin **learning to write capital letters that are made with slanting lines.** Ask, "Who can remember the names of the **two different kinds of slanting lines?**" (Backward- and forward-slanting lines.) **Have one of the children** come to the blackboard, **draw the lines, and name** them as he does so.

Have another child go to the blackboard and **draw the small letter** *x*. Ask the class to tell you what kind of lines it is made up of. Then explain that **the capital letter *X* is made very much like the small** *x*, only bigger. Ask, "Who can tell us how big capital letters are?" (Two spaces high.)

Demonstrate the capital letter *X*, giving an explanation as you do so. **Show the correct slant** for the lines of the letter and **the proper order of the strokes. The backward-slanting line is made first and then the forward-slanting line.** The forward-slanting line crosses over the backward-slanting line on the middle line.

Have the children **practice** the letter a few times **at the blackboard** and then send them to their seats to **proceed with the lesson** according to the directions.

Further Helps for the Teacher

It is important for the children to remember that **the lines of the letter *X* should always cross at the middle.** Be sure to drill this into your children.

Pay close attention to the material covered in the review section, which you will notice is being reintroduced in this lesson. Watch your children's work here to see how they have maintained their ability to make letters or numerals previously learned.

If you have time, you may want to explain to the children that **the capital letter *X* is not used often in words.** This is why we need to use an uncommon word such as *Xenia* for a practice word. Pronounce it for them (zē′nē ə), and explain that it is the name of a city in Ohio.

Lesson 75
Capital Letter A

Lesson 75

Capital Letter A

53

Aim of the Lesson

To teach the formation of the capital letter *A*.

Directions

The children should trace over the strokes and letters in row one. In row two they should practice the letter *A*. In row three the word *Adam* should be traced over and copied once. The children should fill in the remaining space in this row with capital letter *A*'s. Row four is a review row. The children should trace over and copy the letter *F* and the numeral 7 in the space following.

Conducting the Class

Have one child go to the blackboard and **draw the capital letter** *X*, which was learned in the previous lesson.

Be sure you have the attention of the entire class. Then **print a capital letter** *A* on the blackboard, near the capital *X*. Ask the children if they can **see anything that is the same** about the two letters. The similarity is that **both letters contain a backward-slanting line and a forward-slanting line.** Show the children that if you take the two slanting lines of the capital letter *X* apart until their top points touch, you have the framework for the letter *A*. So in this way the two letters are related.

Proceed with an **explanation and a demonstration of the letter** *A*, keeping it as interesting as possible. Have the children name the one stroke in the letter that is not a slanting stroke. Next give instruction in relation to the order of strokes in the letter, which is the reverse of the order in which they are made in the capital letter *X*. In the capital letter *A,* **the forward-slanting line is made first and then the backward-slanting line.** Finally **the across line is made** a short distance below the middle line, going from the forward-slanting line to the backward-slanting line.

Have the children go to the **blackboard** and **practice** the letter on their own. **The first time around have them form the letter with you,** naming each stroke as it is made. Then have them make several more.

The children should **proceed with the lesson** according to the directions when you feel they have practiced the letter sufficiently to make it accurate.

Further Help for the Teacher

Some of your children may have **trouble getting the across line of the letter** *A* **spaced properly up and down.** They shall put it only a short distance below the middle line, neither halfway down to the bottom line nor right at the middle line.

Help your children to **keep the slanting lines of the letter slanted correctly** so that the letter is neither too spread apart nor too narrow and squeezed together.

Do not fail to check the children's spacing or words and letters from time to time. The practice words are given primarily for the purpose of teaching and checking spacing. The children should be taught in each lesson to space each capital letter right, and reminded to space the small letters correctly too.

Lesson 76
Capital Letter N

Lesson 76

Capital Letter N

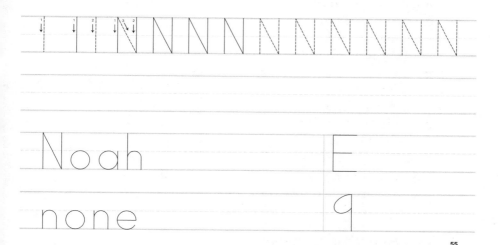

55

Aim of the Lesson

To teach the formation of the capital letter *N*.

Directions

The children should trace over the strokes and letters in row one. In row two they should practice the letter *N*. In rows three and four, the words *Noah* and *none* should each be traced over and copied once. The capital letter *E* and the numerals *9* are reviewed at the end of rows three and four. The children should trace over these and then copy them to the end of each row.

Conducting the Class

Begin the class period by asking this question about the man Noah. "What are some of the things the Bible says Noah did?"

Ask the children what letter the word *Noah* **begins with.** Explain that this is the letter they will be learning today.

Draw the capital letter *N* on the blackboard. Ask the children if they can think of a capital letter they learned not too long ago that looks a lot like the capital *N*. If they cannot think of the right one, **draw the letter** *H* on the blackboard **right beside the letter** *N*. Ask them to tell you how the two letters are alike. **Both letters have two down lines.** The difference between the two is that the letter *H* has an across line in the same space that the letter *N* has a backward-slanting line.

Explain and demonstrate on the blackboard **the order of strokes** of the letter *N*. Begin by giving the order of the **two down strokes,** and explain that the distance between these two strokes is the same as with the capital letter *H*. **The third stroke is the backward-slanting line.** It is made between the top of the first down line and the bottom of the second down line. The pencil must be lifted between each stroke if the letter is to be made right.

Have the children **practice the letter on the blackboard** and then go to their seats to **proceed with the lesson** according to the directions.

Further Helps for the Teacher

Your children will have **problems with the slanting line** of the letter *N*. In aiming on a slant at a point that far away, they will probably have a few **weaves in their lines.** Since this is to be expected, warn them of it beforehand and demonstrate the right way to do it. However, do not be too displeased if there is some weave in the line, unless it is quite drastic. Of course, after some time, you should see some improvement in the formation of this letter. A good time to see how they are coming along with it is several lessons hence when this letter is reviewed.

Do not allow the children to make the letter *N* **without lifting the pencil.** (This will more likely happen later on.) It may seem simpler to make it in a zigzag fashion (**N**), but legibility will be sacrificed by so doing.

As has already been noticed, **the capital H and the capital N are made similarly.** You may also notice that there is a similarity between the small letter h and the small letter n. In each case, only one line is made differently; the basic structure is the same.

Lesson 77
Capital Letter Z

Lesson 77

Capital Letter Z

Z Z Z Z Z Z Z Z Z Z Z

Zion   I

zero   8

57

Aim of the Lesson

To teach the formation of the capital letter *Z*.

Directions

The children should trace over the strokes and letters in row one. In row two, a practice row, the children should fill the row with the letter *Z*. In rows three and four, the words *Zion* and *zero* should be traced over and copied one time each. The letter *I* and the numeral *8* should be traced over and copied in the allotted space.

Conducting the Class

Have the children go to the blackboard. **Review the capital letter** *N* **by giving them a counting drill** on the letter.

When the children are back at their seats, **introduce the letter** *Z*. Ask them if they remember what insect makes the sound of the letter *Z*. (A bee.)

Ask one child to come to the blackboard and draw the small letter *z* beside the capital letter *Z*, naming each stroke.

Explain the formation of the capital letter *Z*. Show that it is made with **the very same strokes as the small letter** *z*, but each is longer to make a capital letter instead of a small letter.

The strokes of the letter *Z* are made as follows: **First, an across line is made along the top line.** Next, without lifting the pencil, **draw a forward-slanting line to the bottom line.** It should end right below the beginning of the across line. What letter or numeral do you have now? The children should be quick to see that it is the numeral 7. However, there is one more line to be drawn, **the across line along the bottom line.** Again without lifting the pencil, draw the across line to a point directly below the end of the top across line.

Have the children **practice the letter on the blackboard** until they have learned to make it well. Then have them go to their seats and **proceed with the lesson,** while you check their work. Be sure they have **correct posture** before they begin.

Further Helps for the Teacher

If you look back to the lesson on the formation of the small letter *z* (**Lesson 32**), you will notice **there are some helps there that apply also to the formation of the capital letter** *Z* because of the similarity of the two letters. You should note that the length of the across lines in the capital letter should be approximately five-eighths inch with a one-inch ruling.

You should also note that **the forward-slanting line does not need to slant quite as much as it does with the small letter** *z* because it is a much taller letter and the across lines are not proportionately longer in relation to the height of the letter.

Lesson 78
Capital Letter K

Lesson 78

Capital Letter K

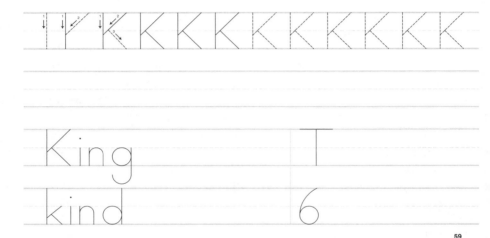

59

Aim of the Lesson

To teach the formation of the capital letter *K*.

Directions

The children should trace over the strokes and letters in row one. In row two, a practice row, the children should fill the space with capital *K*'s. In rows three and four, the children should trace over the words *King* and *kind* and copy each word once in the space following. The letter *T* and the numeral *6* should also be traced over and copied in the space following.

216

Conducting the Class

Begin the class period by asking these questions:

"Can you think of the name of a king in the Bible?" (David, Solomon, Saul, and so forth.)

"What is the name of the king that rules all of heaven and earth?" (God or Jesus.)

"The word *King* begins with what letter?" (*K*; be sure the word is printed on the blackboard so that they can see that it is a capital letter.)

Compare briefly the capital and small letter *k*, but do not go into too much detail, as with this letter it could tend to be confusing.

Have the children help you in the explanation and demonstration of the strokes of the letter. **Ask them questions** to help them identify the different strokes and their order. **The first stroke is a down line** from the top line to the bottom line. **The second stroke is a forward-slanting line,** which starts at the top line out some distance from the top of the down line (show them on the blackboard just where). It should be aimed at a point on the down line just below the middle line. The **third stroke is a backward-slanting line.** It starts at the second stroke where it crosses the middle line. From there it slants to the bottom line. When you are finished with the letter, **the beginning of the second stroke should be directly above the end of the third stroke,** so that a straight line could be drawn down the right side.

Send the children to the **board to practice** the letter on lines which you have drawn for them. This is a letter that will take some practice, so be sure they get enough.

After they have learned the letter fairly well, send them to their seats to **work the lesson** according to the directions.

Further Helps for the Teacher

In this lesson be especially patient with your children. The letter *K* is one of the most difficult letters to write accurately because of the indefinite beginning and ending of the second stroke and the indefinite ending of the third stroke. Also, if the second stroke is made incorrectly, the third one will be made incorrectly too.

The second stroke is the most difficult stroke in this letter. The children will have problems knowing just where to start and what angle to make it. The key is to show correct form by example and then to **give the children plenty of practice.** Be on hand to help them as they practice.

Do not fail to **give a word of praise as needed** to the child who has finally achieved a consistently accurate letter. This will be a real encouragement, especially to one who has previously been frustrated.

Lesson 79
Capital Letter M

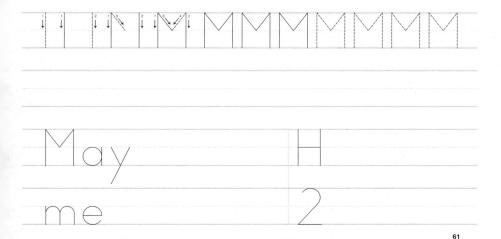

Lesson 79

Capital Letter M

61

Aim of the Lesson

To teach the formation of the capital letter *M*.

Directions

The children should trace over the strokes and letters in row one. In row two they should practice the letter *M*. In rows three and four, the words *May* and *me* should be traced over and copied once. The letter *H* and the numeral *2* should also be traced over and copied in the space allotted.

Conducting the Class

For some variety, you may **teach the children the letter** *M* **according to the following pattern,** if desired:

1. Do not let the children get out their books. **Draw lines for them on the blackboard.**
2. **Send them to the blackboard.** Be sure they each have a piece of chalk and an eraser.
3. **Have them draw the capital letter** *N* neatly and carefully. (You draw along with them so that they have something to refer to if they do not understand the directions.)
4. Explain: **"We are going to change the letter** *N* **to another letter.** Listen carefully while I tell you what to do."
5. "Very carefully **erase the backward-slanting line** with one corner of your eraser. Try not to erase any other lines."
6. **"Draw a down line on the outside of the last down line** of the letter *N*. It should be just a short distance away from the down line and go from the top line to the bottom line."
7. **"Erase the old line** that you drew the new line beside, again very carefully."
8. **"Put your chalk at the top of the first down line. Look at the middle line between the two down lines and try to imagine a spot halfway between. Bring your chalk down** to touch that imaginary spot. What kind of line have you made?" (Backward-slanting.)
9. "Put your **chalk at the top of the second down line. Draw another slanting line to the same spot.** Now what kind of line have you drawn?" (Forward-slanting.)
10. "Who can tell me **what letter we have made?"** (*M*.)

Give the children the order of strokes and then have them **practice the letter** several times on the board. Have them go back to their desks and **proceed with the lesson** according to the directions.

Further Helps for the Teacher

Your children will likely have **difficulty getting the slanting lines to meet exactly in the middle.** This is so because of the difficulty of guessing just exactly where the middle is, especially for a child who is not familiar with the letter. This will come with practice

220

and by correction from the teacher.

Try to be sure that your children keep the down lines of the letter *M* farther apart than the letter *N* *so as* **not to get the letter too crowded.**

Lesson 80
Capital Letter Y

Lesson 80

Capital Letter Y

Yes   X

key   3

63

Aim of the Lesson

To teach the formation of the capital letter *Y*.

Directions

The strokes and letters in row one should be traced over. In row two, the children should practice the letter *Y*. In rows three and four, the words *Yes* and *key* should be traced over and then copied once. The letter *X* and the numeral *3* should also be traced over and copied in the space following.

Conducting the Class

After the children have opened their books, **demonstrate** on the blackboard **how to change the letter** M **to the letter** Y. Let the children look at the letter, compare it with the letter M, and see if they can tell you what to do.

The change is very simple: **Erase the two down lines on each side** of the letter M. **Put a down line at the bottom of the slanting-line combination.**

Ask one of the children to name the strokes of the letter Y. They are **backward-slanting line, forward-slanting line, down line.**

Explain the formation of the letter in this way:

"The top part of the letter is made first. It looks much like a spread-out letter v, only it is between the top and middle lines rather than between the middle and bottom lines. **The backward-slanting line is made first,** from the top line to the middle line. **The forward-slanting line comes next.** It should start at the top line out some distance and slant back and down to touch the middle line at the same spot as does the backward-slanting line. For the last **stroke** of the letter, the pencil is placed at the point **where the two slanting lines join, and a down line is drawn straight to the bottom line."**

Send the children to the **blackboard** to **practice** the letter on lines which you have drawn for them. Then have the children come back to their seats and **proceed with the lesson** according to the directions.

Further Helps for the Teacher

Notice how the letter Y is spaced. The top of the letter is spread out and the bottom is narrow, so **the next letter will need to be spaced from the top of the letter** Y, as demonstrated by the letter e in the word *Yes.*

There is some difference between the top of the letter Y and the letter v, but your children may not be able to see it. The top of Y is wider (about three-fourths inch with a one-inch ruling), while v is narrower (one-half inch with a one-inch ruling). **Teach the letter correctly by helping them think of** Y **as being made from** M **rather than from** v. Then, if you see a Y on one of your children's papers that is too narrow, draw a down line on each side and ask, "How does it look when it is used to make the letter *M*?"

Be sure the three strokes all join accurately, with no gaps, overlaps, or offsets at the point of joining.

Lesson 81
Capital Letter V

Lesson 81

Capital Letter $\lor$

Very   A

vow   5

65

Aim of the Lesson

To teach the formation of the capital letter *V*.

Directions

The children should trace over the strokes and letters in row one. In row two they should practice the letter *V*. In rows three and four, the words *Very* and *vow* should be traced over and copied once. The letter *A* and the numeral *5* should also be traced over and copied in the space following.

225

Conducting the Class

Send the children to the **blackboard to review the letters** Y **and** M. Have them print at least five of each.

Have the children return to their seats. **Introduce the capital letter** V by drawing it on the blackboard. **Draw the small letter** v **beside it for comparison.** Show them that the capital letter is similar in appearance to the small letter but it is twice as tall.

Ask the children to tell you **the two strokes of the letter.** They are the **backward-slanting line** and the **forward-slanting line.**

Explain to the children that to make the letter V, the two slanting lines should **begin the same distance apart as the slanting lines of the letter** Y. But instead of drawing each line to a point on the middle line, you **draw each line to a point on the bottom line.**

Have the children practice the letter V on lines you have drawn for them on the blackboard. Start out by having them practice the letter carefully for accuracy and then **give them a counting drill on the letter.**

Send the children back to their seats to **do the lesson** according to the directions.

Further Helps for the Teacher

The biggest catch with this letter is its **long, slanting lines,** which **will make accuracy in aiming rather difficult** for your children. Do not be surprised to see a few wavers in the lines.

As with the letter Y, you will need **to be sure that the lines meet accurately at the point of joining.**

You will notice that the letter V has a steeper slant than any letter learned so far. **Be sure the slants do not get too slanted,** or it will make the letter too wide at the top.

This letter, again, is one that **needs to be properly spaced, from the top** and not from the bottom. Be sure the children space it correctly.

Lesson 82
Capital Letter W

Lesson 82

Capital Letter W

W W W W W W W W W W

West

N

win

O

67

Aim of the Lesson

To teach the formation of the capital letter *W*.

Directions

The strokes and letters in row one are to be traced over. Row two is for practice of the letter *W*. In rows three and four, the words *West* and *win* should be traced over and copied once. The letter *N* and the numeral *0* should also be traced over and copied in the allotted space.

Conducting the Class

Begin the class period by **drawing a capital letter** W **on the blackboard.** Beside it, **draw the small letter** w **for comparison.** Next ask the children to name **two kinds of strokes** that are used in this letter. They are the **backward-slanting line and the forward-slanting line,** the same as in the letter V.

Move on into the demonstration and explanation of the letter W. Explain each stroke as follows:

First stroke —starts at the top line
       —is a **backward-slanting line;**
       —goes to the bottom line.

Second stroke —starts at the top line (show where);
       —is a **forward-slanting line;**
       —touches the bottom line at the end of the first stroke.

Third stroke —starts at the top of the second stroke at the top line;
       —is a **backward-slanting line;**
       —goes to the bottom line.

Fourth stroke —starts at the top line (show where);
       —is a **forward-slanting line;**
       —touches the bottom line at the end of the third stroke.

Send the children to the **blackboard** to **practice** this letter. Give a **counting drill** on the letter as you did the letter V. Count one number for each stroke.

At their seats, the children should **proceed with the lesson** according to the above directions. Check on their posture before they begin.

Further Helps for the Teacher

The letter W **will give you an opportunity to help correct any errors the children may have been making in forming the letter** V, since the two letters are made similarly. One example of an area that may need help is accurate joining of slanting strokes in such a way that they meet exactly, without offsets, gaps, or overlaps.

The lines of the letter W **do not slant as much as do the lines of the letter** V. Show the children by example just how much the lines do slant, without making a special point of this.

Be sure the children begin all their strokes at the top line and go down. Making a letter as tall as this one in a zigzag fashion is almost certain to result in a poor copy.

Lesson 83
Making Words With Capitals

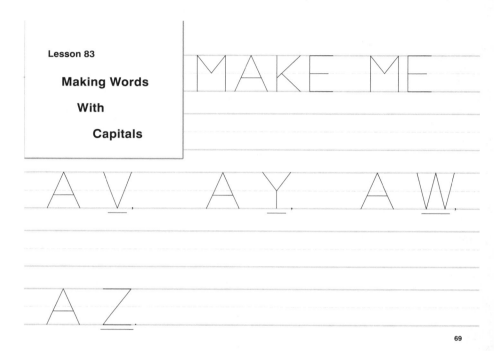

Aim of the Lesson

To teach the children the spacing of capital letters within a word written entirely with capitals; to relate words made with capitals to their common usage; to review the letters *Z, K, M, Y, V,* and *W*; and to give a brief introduction to the writing of sentences.

Directions

The children should trace over all the words and letters in rows one, three, and five. Next have them copy rows one and three in the spaces directly below in rows two and four. The beginning of row five should be copied in the space at the end of the same row.

Conducting the Class

Print the word *MAN* **on the blackboard** in capital letters. Ask the children:

"What is different about the word *MAN* **as written here** from other words we have written? **[It is written entirely with capitals.]** Have you seen words or groups of words written in this way anywhere else?"

Explain to the children that one place where they possibly can find words written entirely with capital letters is textbook covers. Pick out a textbook with the title and author's name in capital letters, and show it to them.

Try to get across to the children that the important thing in writing words with all capitals is getting the spacing right. The children are not used to spacing one capital from another; rather, small letters from capital letters and small letters from each other. Teach them that **when writing with all capitals, the letters should be spaced a little farther apart** than when small letters are being spaced. **Demonstrate** the difference in spacing.

Send the children to the **blackboard** and have them **practice** several words to be written with all capital letters. Be sure to use words that can be made using only the straight-line and slant-line capitals learned thus far. Here are some words that can be used: *THE, LINE, MAN, MAY,* and *HIM.*

As the children open their books to the lesson, **explain to them** that in this lesson they will not only be writing words, but **the words will be put together to form a sentence.** Read the sentence to them: "Make me a *V*, a *Y*, a *W*, a *Z*." (This sentence is given as though the teacher is asking the children to write these letters.) Tell the children to put in the commas within the sentence, underline the letters indicated, and place the period at the end. Then **have them proceed with the lesson** according to the directions. Be sure the children are **holding their pencils correctly** and **exercising correct posture.**

Further Helps for the Teacher

As the children make their capital letters, check their formation of each one, especially the letters *Z, K, M, Y, V,* and *W.* This is the first review of these letters since they were originally learned.

Look especially for improvement in the straightness of long, slanting lines as noted in Lesson 76.

Lesson 84
Review of Slant-line Capitals

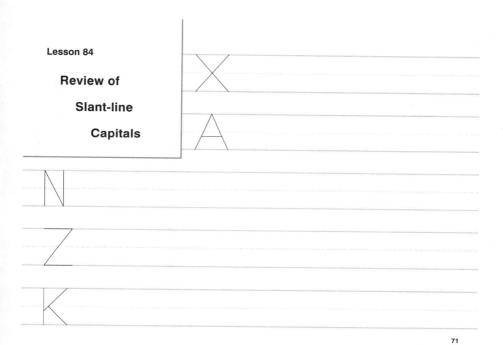

Lesson 84

Review of

Slant-line

Capitals

71

Aim of the Lesson

To thoroughly review the capital letters *X, A, N, Z, K, M, Y, V,* and *W.*

Directions

In each row that begins with a capital letter, the children should trace over each figure and copy it until the row is filled. In the last line on the second page, have the children practice the manuscript strokes as you give out the name of each stroke.

233

Conducting the Class

Explain to the children that this lesson is to make sure they have really learned the last nine letters studied. **Ask the children, "What kind of letters have we been learning?" (Capital letters made with slanting lines.)**

Have the children give orally the **stroke combinations of each of the letters.** They are as follows:

X—b-s line, f-s line

A—f-s line, b-s line, across line

N—down line, down line, b-s line

Z—across line, f-s line, across line

K—down line, f-s line, b-s line

M—down line, down line, b-s line, f-s line

Y—b-s line, f-s line, down line

V—b-s line, f-s line

W—b-s line, f-s line, b-s line, f-s line

The following questions test the children's ability to differentiate between letters by their strokes and qualities. **Ask the children these questions** to be answered orally:

"How many of the slant-line letters that we have learned are two spaces high?" (All of them.)

"Which letters have both backward- and forward-slanting lines?" (*X, A, K, M, Y, V,* and *W.*)

"Which letter has no backward-slanting line?" (*Z.*)

"Which letter has no forward-slanting line?" (*N.*)

"Which letters have across lines?" (*A, Z.*)

"Which letters have one down line?" (*K, Y.*)

"Which letters have two down lines?" (*N, M.*)

"Which letter has slanting lines that cross each other in the middle?" (*X.*)

Have the children practice each letter on the blackboard until you are satisfied with their performance. Then they can go to their seats and **proceed with the lesson** according to the directions.

Further Helps for the Teacher

If time is at a premium, some of the questions above could be omitted.

Are your children still able to form and space accurately the six letters that are formed with straight lines?

You should see that the children are meeting the following standards and goals learned from the last ten lessons:

1. **They should be able to form accurately and neatly the nine letters reviewed in this lesson.**
2. They should be able to make slanted lines that are of the correct slant for each letter (at least very nearly so).
3. **They should be able to make their slanted lines join accurately,** without gaps, overlaps, or offsets.
4. **They should be able to space the capital letters learned in relation to small letters, as well as to other capital letters.**

Lesson 85
Capital Letter O

Lesson 85

Capital Letter ○

Obed   LET

obey

73

Aim of the Lesson

To teach the formation of the capital letter *O*.

Directions

The children should trace over the stroke and letters in row one. In row two, they should practice the letter *O*. In rows three and four, have them trace over the words *Obed* and *obey* and copy each one time. They should trace over the word *LET* in row three and copy it in the space below in row four.

236

Conducting the Class

Draw the letter _O_ on the blackboard. Ask the children, "What letter or numeral that we have already learned looks exactly like this letter?" (The numeral _0._) Explain to them that **the letter _O_ looks exactly the same as the numeral _0_.** The reason is that **both of them are made up of one large circle stroke. Demonstrate** by writing the number _10_ on blackboard beside the letter _O_ that you have written.

Since the children no doubt still need practice on the **large circle stroke, it would be good to spend much of this class period practicing this stroke,** both on the blackboard and on paper. Make use of the practice paper in the book. Also, it would be a good time to pay attention to some other miscellaneous areas related to handwriting. Ask these questions: "How are my **left-handed students** coming along?" What about the **line quality** of the children's writing? Is their writing too light or too heavy? Do they maintain **correct posture and pencil-holding habits** nearly automatically, without always needing to be reminded?" Following the practice period, have the children **proceed with the lesson** at their seats according to the directions.

Further Helps for the Teacher

Some of the children may not be familiar with the name _Obed._ Explain that he was Ruth's son and King David's grandfather.

As your children again practice **the circle form, you will find that they have by no means perfected it yet.** It will likely be some time before they do. But do not be discouraged. And do not stop short of the goal of having your students achieve a good circle form. Continue emphasizing strongly the principles of circle formation, and insist that the children practice the circle, keeping these principles in mind. If you keep at it, eventually you will find that you have achieved your goal.

You will need to be careful not to insist too hard on perfection **now** in a certain area of writing, if the child is already doing the best he can. **Remember that learning takes time.** Pushing a child to do what he is not yet able to do will frustrate both you and him.

A better approach is to gently remind the child where he can improve, and give him some positive helps. If the child cannot do as well as you would like now, let him do the best he can, set it aside, and come back to it later.

Lesson 86
Capital Letter Q

Lesson 86

Capital Letter Q

Aim of the Lesson

To teach the formation of the capital letter *Q*.

Directions

The children should trace over the strokes and letters in row one. In row two they should practice the letter *Q*. In rows three and four, have the children trace over the words *Queen* and *quick* and then copy each word once. Have the children fill the space at the end of the fourth row with capital *O*'s.

Conducting the Class

The most obvious thing that you will want your children to notice about **the letter Q is its similarity to the letter 0.** They should have no difficulty at all in understanding how this letter is to be made.

Place both letters side by side on the blackboard. Show that the letter **Q has an extra stroke,** in the lower right-hand corner, that crosses the circle. Ask the children to tell you what kind of stroke it is. **It is a backward-slanting line** that begins inside the circle, crosses the circle, and ends at the bottom line.

Also compare the capital letter Q with the small letter q, showing the children that there is almost no similarity between the two.

Have the children **practice the letter Q on the blackboard.** Following this practice, have them go to their seats and **proceed with the lesson** according to the directions.

Further Helps for the Teacher

Try to get the children to **make the stroke cross the circle as near at right angles as possible.** Also they should try to have about the **same amount of line on the inside as on the outside of the circle** and have the line **cross at the right place on the circle.** Finally, be sure that the second stroke touches the bottom line.

In this lesson the children will again have the opportunity to practice the formation of the large circle stroke. Be aware of this so that you can continue to help those whose circles are inaccurate.

Lesson 87
Capital Letter C

Lesson 87

Capital Letter C

CCCCCCCCCC

Cain   Q

can

77

Aim of the Lesson

To teach the formation of the capital letter C.

Directions

The children should trace over the stroke and letters in row one and then practice them in row two. In rows three and four, they should trace over the words *Cain* and *can* and then copy each word. The children should use the space left in rows three and four to practice the letter Q.

Conducting the Class

Print the letter C on the blackboard. Ask the children to tell you **what kind of stroke** is used in forming the letter C. (**A part-circle or curve** stroke.) So the letter C is actually part of a large circle.

To demonstrate the above, **draw a large circle on the blackboard. Erase the part not needed,** to show how the letter C is formed from a large circle.

You should also show the children the similarity between the capital letter C and the small letter c. **Show that the small letter is a small curve and that the capital letter is a large curve.**

Demonstrate to the children **just where the stroke forming the letter C is to begin and end. Explain it this way:**

"The letter C begins at exactly the same place as the letter O. Begin the letter by starting to make a large circle. Touch the top line, continue drawing around and down to the bottom line and then up a short distance. The end of the curve should be the same distance from the bottom line as the starting point is from the top line. The ending point should also be directly below the starting point."

Have the children go to the **blackboard** and **practice** the letter until you are satisfied that they are making it the best they can. Then have them **proceed with the lesson** according to the directions.

Further Helps for the Teacher

You may remember from the lesson about the small letter c that this letter is one of the more difficult to make. The capital letter C is even more difficult because of the large size of the curve. **The children may tend not to curve out far enough on the back side of the letter,** or **they might tend to put corners on the curve at various locations.** You will need to watch their formations closely and give help where it is needed.

Lesson 88
Capital Letter G

Lesson 88

Capital Letter G

C C G G G G G G G

God   C

gave

79

Aim of the Lesson

To teach the formation of the capital letter *G*.

Directions

The children should trace over the strokes and letters in row one. In row two, they should practice the letter *G*. In rows three and four, the words *God* and *gave* should be traced over and then copied at least once each. The letter *c* should be traced over and then copied in the space at the end of rows three and four.

Conducting the Class

In teaching the formation of the letter *G*, you can **build it upon the letter** *C*, since the form of *C* is a part of the letter *G*.

First **have the children** come to the blackboard and **draw the letter** *C*. Then **show them how they can make the letter** *G* **from the letter** *C*. From the end of the letter *C*, they should draw a short **up line,** ending just below the middle line. Next they should lift the chalk and draw a short **across line** on top of the up line. When finished, it will look like the letter *C* with a very small *T* at the end.

Have them draw several of the letter *G* following the above procedure. The children can be helped to recall the formation of the letter *G* by remembering that it is made up of a letter *C* plus an up line and an across line. Explain that **the across line is not to be made too long and that there should be an equal amount of line on each side of the up line.**

When the children return to their seats, **call their attention to the strokes shown at the beginning of row one,** showing them that these strokes are like the strokes that they drew on the blackboard. Finally, have them **proceed with the lesson** after you have given proper directions.

Further Helps for the Teacher

Call the children's attention to the words in the lesson: "God gave." Discuss what God's most precious gift to us is.

You should **help the children not to make the joining point too sharp between the curve and the up line.** They should round the point slightly, yet not so much that the up line is totally indistinguishable from the curve. Use your own judgment on the degree of sharpness necessary to make a neat-looking letter.

The **up line should not come up to the middle line.** If it does, the across line will fade into the middle line and the letter will be more easily confused with the letter *C*.

Be sure the children's across lines touch the top of the up line.

Lesson 89
Capital Letter S

Lesson 89

Capital Letter S

S S S S S S S S S S S S

Satan

sin   G

81

Aim of the Lesson

To teach the formation of the capital letter S.

Directions

The children should trace over the strokes and letters in row one. The letter S should be practiced in row two. In rows three and four the words *Satan* and *sin* should be traced over and then copied once. The letter G should be traced over and copied in the space following.

Conducting the Class

In introducing the letter *S,* **compare it with the numeral** *8.* Draw the numeral *8* on the blackboard and erase the last stroke to show the similarity.

Explain that the same basic motions are used in making the letter *S* as in making the first part of the numeral *8.* **Both begin at the same place and go around in the same direction.** The only difference is that the slant between the double curves is steeper in the numeral *8* than in the letter *S.* **Demonstrate** these facts on the blackboard.

You should also **show your children the similarities between the capital letter** *S* **and the small letter** *s.* Their formations are identical, except that the small letter *s* is only half the height and size of the capital letter.

Explain to the children that there are two strokes in the letter *S.* **One is a curve in one direction, and the other is a curve in the other direction.** The letter begins at the normal place for a small circle, a short distance below the top line. It curves back up to the top line and then around and down to the middle line. At the middle line, it begins to curve in the opposite direction, curves forward and down, and then back to the bottom line. Continue curving until the line is as far above the bottom line as the beginning point of the letter is below the top line.

Have the children go to the **blackboard** and **practice** the letter a number of times. Following this practice, they should go to their seats and **proceed with the lesson** after you have given them directions.

Further Helps for the Teacher

Make an association in the children's minds between *Satan* and *sin,* the two words in the lesson. Satan causes people to sin, or to disobey God.

Since the two forms of the letter *s* are basically made the same, by and large the problem associated with forming the small letter will apply to the capital letter also (see Lesson 43). However, you have one aid with the capital letter that you did not have with the small letter, and that is the middle line. **This line provides a reference point in making the letter that will simplify its formation** for the children.

Lesson 90
Capital Letter D

Lesson 90

Capital Letter D

Aim of the Lesson

To teach the formation of the capital letter *D*.

Direction

The strokes and letters in row one should be traced over. The letter *D* should be practiced in row two. In rows three and four the children should trace over the words *David* and *did* and then copy each once. The children should trace over and copy the letter *S* in the space at the end of row four.

Conducting the Class

Send the children to the blackboard to review the letter *S*. Have them return to their seats; then **draw a capital** *D* **on the blackboard.** Now **ask** the children **how many strokes they think the letter** *D* **has.** They may say two. Explain to them that **actually the letter** *D* **has four different strokes** but **three of them are put together** in such a way that you hardly know where one stops and the next one starts.

Demonstrate and explain the formation of the letter as follows, asking the children questions to keep them with you:

"**The first stroke, a down line,** is drawn from the top line to the bottom line. Next the pencil is lifted and placed at the top of the down line. Now **the next three strokes are all drawn in one motion. A short across line** is drawn forward. **This is the second** stroke. The **third stroke is a large curve** that makes a half-circle. It curves from the end of the across line forward, down, and back to the bottom line. When the curve reaches the bottom line, the **fourth stroke begins.** It is an across line that goes straight back to the bottom of the down line. The letter is finished."

Have the children come again to the **blackboard** and **practice** the letter before they **go ahead with the lesson.**

Further Helps for the Teacher

At the beginning, you will want to have the children stop briefly at the ends of the second and third strokes so that they understand the place and value of each stroke. But once this is understood, **help them blend the two across lines and the curve together smoothly** in one continuous motion.

Sometimes children's letter *D*'s **look like this (D), with the curve coming in too fast and sharp** rather than going out around as it should. When this happens, the fourth stroke is eliminated entirely and the *D* does not have a pleasing appearance. So be sure that the children's curve lines curve out far enough so that there is sufficient room for the fourth stroke at the end.

Be sure that the two across lines join accurately with the down line so that there are no gaps, offsets, or overlaps.

Have you been keeping an eye on your children's **posture and pencil-holding** habits?

Lesson 91
Capital Letter P

Lesson 91

Capital Letter P

P P P P P P P P P P P

Paul   D

pen

85

Aim of the Lesson

To teach the formation of the capital letter *P*.

Directions

The children should trace over the strokes and letters in row one. They should practice the letter *P* in row two. In rows three and four, the words *Paul* and *pen* should be traced over and then copied one time each. The letter *D* should be traced over and copied at the end of rows three and four.

Conducting the Class

Introduce **the letter *P* by drawing it on the blackboard.** Ask the children to tell you have many strokes are in this letter. **Like the letter *D*, it is made up of four strokes.**

Explain to the children that in many ways the letter *P* is like the letter *D*. **Draw the letter *D* beside the letter *P* and compare them.** Instead of a large curve that goes all the way to the bottom line, the letter *P* has a small curve that only goes to the middle line. The across lines of *P* are also somewhat longer.

Demonstrate and explain the formation of the letter as follows:

"**The first stroke is a down line** from the top line to the bottom line. **The second stroke** begins at the top of the down line and **goes across** for a short distance. **The third stroke is a curve** that curves down from the end of the across line to the middle line. When the curve reaches the middle line, it changes to **the fourth stroke, which is an across line.** It travels along the middle line back to the down line."

Have the children **practice this letter on the blackboard.** Give them directions for the lesson and then have them proceed with it.

Further Helps for the Teacher

Watch for improper spacing between the letter *P* and short letters that follow. The tendency may be to print the short letter too close to the letter *P*.

Be sure that **the across lines of the letter *P* are made longer than the across lines of the letter *D*.**

Again you will want to **help your children blend the strokes together** well. Try to help them make a smooth, round curve. Do not allow them to make one round curve for the last three strokes of the letter, thereby omitting one or more of the across lines.

Lesson 92
Capital Letter R

Lesson 92

Capital Letter R

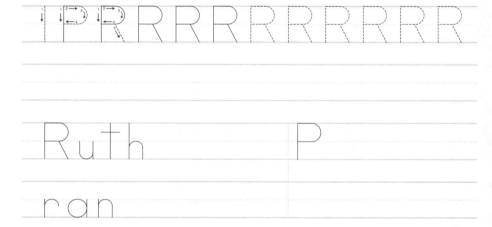

87

Aim of the Lesson

To teach the formation of the capital letter R.

Directions

The children should trace over the strokes and letters in row one. In row two, the letter R should be practiced. In rows three and four, the words *Ruth* and *ran* should be traced over and copied once. The letter P should be traced over and copied in the allotted space at the end of rows three and four.

250

Conducting the Class

Tell the children that today they are going to learn to print the capital letter *R*. Explain that this should be simple if they learned yesterday's letter well, because **the letter *R* is made much like yesterday's letter.** Ask the children, "What was yesterday's letter?" (*P.*)

Have the children give you each stroke of the letter *P* as you draw it on the blackboard. When the letter *P* is finished, **show how the letter *R* is made from it by the addition of a backward-slanting line.** The backward-slanting line begins at the middle line where the third and fourth strokes meet and goes to the bottom line.

Give the children some **practice at the blackboard,** having them print both the letter *P* and the letter *R*.

Before the children actually begin the lesson, call attention to the difference in formation between the capital letter *R* and the small letter *r*. **The children should realize that the two forms of the same letter are made differently.**

At their seats, the children should **proceed with the lesson** according to the directions.

Further Helps for the Teacher

Emphasize to the children **the point where the backward-slanting line joins the rest of the letter.** They should remember that **it is right where the curve stops and the across line begins.**

Also **be sure that the slanted line is slanted correctly.** Especially watch that it does not have too much slant.

Lesson 93
Capital Letter B

Lesson 93

Capital Letter B

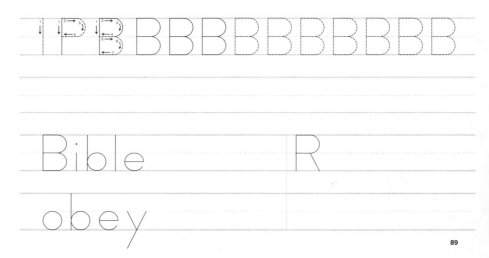

Aim of the Lesson

To teach the formation of the capital letter *B*.

Directions

The children should trace over the strokes and letters in row one. In row two the letter *B* should be practiced. In rows three and four, the words *Bible* and *obey* should be traced over and copied once. The letter *R* should also be traced over and copied in the allotted space at the end of rows three and four.

Conducting the Class

Explain to the children **that the letter** B **is made much like the letter** P **and the letter** R. **Draw the letter** B **on the blackboard.** Show the children that **the bottom part of the letter is identical to the top part** of the letter.

Explain the formation of the letter B as follows:

"The letter consists of **seven different strokes,** but it is made with **only three basic motions.** The first motion is the **down line** that goes from the top line to the bottom line. The next motion is made up of three strokes: an **across line** along the top line, a **curve** down to the middle line, and another **across line** back along the middle line to the down line. Now without lifting your pencil, **the third motion is made, using the same three strokes over again in exactly the same way;** but this time you will go from the middle line to the bottom line."

Also **compare the capital letter** B **with the small letter** b for the children. Show that the **only real similarity is the down line,** which is the first stroke of both letters.

At the **blackboard** have the children **practice** this letter a number of times and then **give them a counting drill** on the letter. Say a number for each *motion* (not for each stroke) of the letter. The children should learn to write the letter in three motions, not seven.

Following the drill, the children should **proceed with the lesson** according to the directions.

Further Helps for the Teacher

Be sure that your children make their curves well-rounded. They may have a tendency to make their circles pointed at the farthest extremity like this (B). You should also **see to it that the across lines are not curved along with the curve.** They should keep their distinction as across lines.

It is important that **the two curves of the letter** B **are well aligned.** A vertical line drawn down the right side should touch the farthest extremity of both curves.

Lesson 94
Capital Letter J

Lesson 94

Capital Letter J

Aim of the Lesson

To teach the formation of the capital letter *J*.

Directions

The children should trace over the strokes and letters in row one. In row two they should practice the letter *J*. In rows three and four, the words *Jesus* and *joy* should be traced over and copied at least once. The letter *B* in row four should also be traced over and copied in the allotted space.

Conducting the Class

Carefully **draw the letter J on the blackboard.** Ask the children to tell you how many and what kind of strokes are to be found in this letter. **There are three strokes.** They are **a down line, a curve, and an across line.**

Explain and demonstrate the formation of the letter J to the children. The letter J begins at the top line with a down line. The down line goes down to about halfway between the middle and the bottom lines. Here a backward curve begins, curving down to the bottom line and then back up halfway to the middle line. A short line like that on capital I finishes the letter. (Also show them the difference between a capital J and a small j.)

At the **blackboard** have the children **practice** the letter J. They should also review the letter B before returning to their seats.

As the children begin their lesson, call their attention to the words *Jesus* and *joy.* Explain that when *Jesus* is with us, we are full of *joy.*

Have the children **proceed with the lesson** after you give the directions.

Further Helps for the Teacher

One area you will need to watch with the letter J is the **common tendency to curve the down line in with the curve.** The down line should maintain its identity as a down line and not be too well blended with the curve.

Do not forget to **check the alignment** of your children's letters frequently. Are their letters resting squarely on the bottom line, and do they touch the middle and upper lines at the proper places?

Lesson 95
Capital Letter U

Lesson 95

Capital Letter U

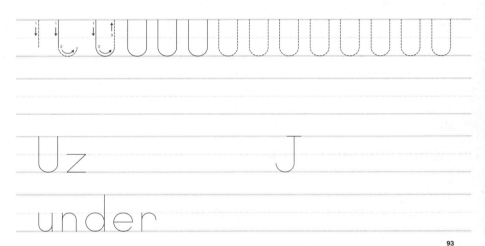

Aim of the Lesson

To teach the formation of the capital letter U.

Directions

The strokes and letters in row one should be traced over. In row two, the children should practice the letter U. In rows three and four, the words Uz and $under$ should be traced over and copied once. The letter J should also be traced over and copied at the end of row three.

Conducting the Class

Tell the children that this is the last letter of the capital letter alphabet that they will be learning. After this they will be practicing all the letters so that they learn to make them better than they can now.

After you have written the letter *U* **on the blackboard,** ask the children to **tell you how many strokes** are in the letter. **There are three: a down line,** a **curve,** and an **up line.**

Explain and demonstrate the formation of the letter as follows:

"The letter *U* **begins with a down line** from the top line to about halfway between the middle and bottom lines. Without lifting your pencil, the **second stroke, a forward curve,** is begun. It curves down to the bottom line and then back up. Again about halfway between the bottom and middle lines, the line stops curving, and the **third stroke, an up line,** is drawn straight to the top line."

Show the children the difference between the capital *U* **and small** *u*.

Have the children go to the **blackboard. They should print the letter** *U* a number of times with your help and supervision.

Following blackboard practice of the letter, have the children go to their seats and **do the lesson** according to the directions.

Further Helps for the Teacher

Check the children's **posture** and **pencil-holding** habits.

With this letter, the children will have the same problem as with the letter *J*, and that is the **tendency to curve the straight lines in with the curve.** This lesson will give you another opportunity to work with your children on this.

The word *Uz* given in the lesson is the name of the land where Job lived. You may want to tell your children this.

Do as much correction as possible at the blackboard, rather than when the children are doing their lesson or working on paper. Watch the important **areas of quality and form** while you have the handwriting right out where it can easily be corrected. You should insist that your children do their very best at the blackboard and then help them to perform on paper as nearly as possible what they were able to do at the board.

Lessons 96 and 97
Review of Circle and Curve Capitals

Aim of the Lessons

To thoroughly review the capital letters *O, Q, C, G, S, D, P, R, B, J,* and *U.*

Directions

In each lesson, the children are to trace over each letter and copy it in the allotted space following.

Conducting the Class

Lesson 96

Explain to the children that **this lesson and the next lesson are review lessons of the last eleven letters learned,** which are the circle and curve capitals.

In this lesson **discuss the stroke combinations** of each of these eleven capital letters. **Draw all eleven of them on the blackboard** so that the children can easily see them.

Look at each letter individually, having the children give the strokes of each letter orally. For a quick rundown of the combinations, they are as follows:

O—large circle

Q—circle, b-s line

C—curve

G—curve, up line, across line

S—curve, curve (double curve)

D—down line, across line, curve, across line

P—down line, across line, curve, across line

R—down line, across line, curve, across line, b-s line

B—down line, across line, curve, across line; across line, curve, across line

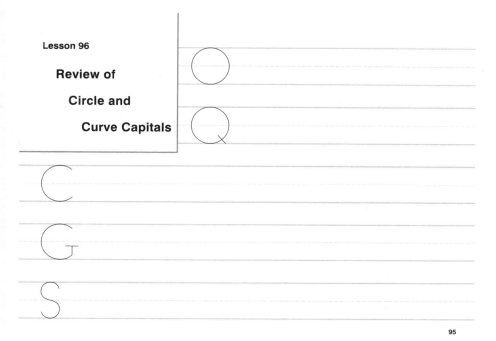

Lesson 96

Review of

Circle and

Curve Capitals

95

J—down line, curve, across line

U—down line, curve, up line

Before the children do the lesson, some **blackboard practice** would be beneficial to them if there is time.

Have the children **proceed to work the lesson.**

Lesson 97

Again, **you should have the eleven capital letters printed on the blackboard.**

In this lesson, **discuss the characteristics of the letters by asking the following questions.** These questions test the children's ability to differentiate letters by their strokes and qualities. Have the children study the letters on the blackboard and answer the questions orally.

"The letters *D* and *P* are made with the same strokes. [Give them]. What then is the difference between the two letters?" (The letter *D* has a large curve; the letter *P* has a small one.

"Which letters are made with circles?" (*O* and *Q.*)

"Which letters are made with large curves?" (*C, G,* and *D.*)

"Which two letters each have a backward-slanting line?" (*Q* and *R.*)

259

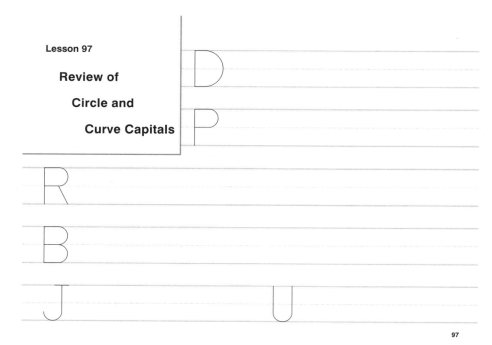

97

"Which two letters have two curves each?" (*S* and *B*.)

"Which letters have down lines?" (*D, P, R, B, J,* and *U*.)

"Which letters have up lines?" (*G* and *U*.)

"Which letters have across lines?" (*G, D, P, R, B,* and *J*.)

Following a discussion of these questions, **have the children proceed with Lesson 97.**

Further Helps for the Teacher

You should make sure that the children are **meeting the following goals** from the last eleven lessons:

1. **They should be able to form accurately and neatly the eleven letters reviewed** in these two lessons.
2. **Their smoothness and accuracy in making both large and small circles and curves should be improving.**
3. Their skills in **properly blending straight lines** with curves should be improving.
4. **They should be able to space the capital letters accurately in relation to the small letters.**

Lesson 98
More Words With Capitals

Lesson 98

More Words

With

Capitals

GOD SAYS

OBEY THE

BIBLE.

99

Aim of the Lesson

To increase the children's understanding of and familiarity with capital letters and to aid them in their proper spacing.

Directions

The children should trace over the words. Those in rows one and three should be copied below in the space in rows two and four. In row five, they should copy the word in the space following.

Conducting the Class

Write the word *OBEY* **in capital letters** on the blackboard. **Discuss the spacing of the letters** in the word. Review with the children the **need for having all the letters equally spaced apart. Also emphasize** that **the spacing between** the **words** be equal and not too small.

Help the children notice the words of the lesson. They should see that **together they express a thought, or make a sentence.** Point out the period. Talk a little about the sentence.

Following instructions, have the children **proceed with the lesson.**

Further Helps for the Teacher

Even though letter form is not being emphasized in these lessons, you should still not forget to work on it as a means of preparation for the unit review lessons.

Go over again with the children some of the uses of words made with all capital letters. They are used for book and lesson titles and to emphasize important words and names. Show them how the name *LORD* is capitalized in the Old Testament.

Lesson 99
More Words With Capitals

Lesson 99

More Words

With

Capitals

JUST DO

WHAT IS

RIGHT.

101

Aim of the Lesson

To improve the children's understanding of, familiarity with, and proper spacing of capital letters.

Directions

The children should trace over each word printed. Rows one and three should be copied in the space below in rows two and four. The word in row five should be copied in the space following.

Conducting the Class

For a blackboard exercise, **have the children write their names and the names of several of their classmates** (not more than five or six) **in capital letters.** They might need help in spelling the names of classmates.

Look at the words in the lesson with the children. Explain that if we do what God says in the Bible (Lesson 98), we will be doing what is right. Everything God tells us in the Bible is the right thing to do. He tells children to obey their parents.

When the children are back at their desks, give them their instructions. **Have them proceed with the lesson.**

Further Helps for the Teacher

While the children are at the blackboard, **check their blackboard-writing habits.** These include their **posture** at the blackboard and **the way they hold and use the chalk.** They should stand with both feet on the floor, back about one foot from the board. The chalk should be held parallel with the fingers, pointing into the palm of the hand. It should not be held like a pencil.

Lesson 100
More Words With Capitals

Lesson 100

More Words

With

Capitals

LOVE TO

BE FAIR AND

KIND.

103

Aim of the Lesson

To further increase the children's understanding and proper spacing of capital letters.

Directions

The children should trace over each word printed. Rows one and three should be copied in the space below in rows two and four. The word in row five should be copied in the space following.

Conducting the Class

For a blackboard exercise, **have the children copy the title of one of their textbooks in capital letters.** (Decide ahead of time what that will be.)

Talk about the relation between the words in this lesson and the words in the last lesson. If we are doing what is right, we will want to be fair and kind to others.

Send the children back to their seats. Have them proceed with the lesson according to directions.

Further Helps for the Teacher

It would be good for you to **look ahead to the next lesson at the goals you are to reach** in the review lessons on capital letters, so that you have a little more time to be sure your children are meeting them.

Lesson 101
Review of Capitals (A–M)

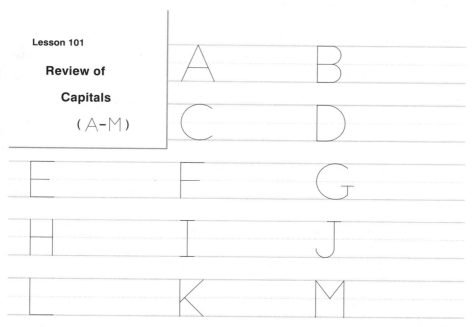

Aim of the Lesson

To review and test the children's understanding of the formation of the first thirteen capital letters of the alphabet.

Directions

The children should trace over each letter and copy it at least twice in the space following.

Conducting the Class

At the beginning of the class period, **have the children go to the blackboard and draw each capital letter** (A–M) with its corresponding small letter beside it.

Briefly discuss each letter. If time permits, ask the children to describe briefly, in their own words, how to make each letter. Encourage them to use the names of the strokes to describe the letter, rather than saying, "Go down here and then around," and so forth.

Check to see which capital letters they need to improve on and have them practice them further either at the blackboard or on paper.

At their seats the children should **proceed with the lesson** according to the instructions. Have them hand in their papers, and then you **evaluate and grade the letters as a test** (see below).

Further Helps for the Teacher

In evaluating these lessons, **check the children's work in the following areas.**

Letter formation: Accuracy is the important thing: no misplaced, missing, or added strokes.

Accuracy in strokes: Are the slants made accurately, within reasonable tolerance of what they should be? Are the curves too shallow or too deep, again within a reasonable tolerance? Are the down lines vertical, or are they slanted?

Joining of strokes: They should be joined with no gaps, overlaps, or offsets.

Smoothness and evenness: Lines should not do much weaving; there should be a minimum of unnecessary jerks and wiggles.

Alignment: the letters should rest on the bottom line (not above or below) and touch the top and middles lines at the proper places.

Grade the children's papers on the basis of acceptability in these areas, not simply on the general appearance of their work.

If desired, you can spend slightly more time the first day and combine Lessons 101 and 102, giving them as review lessons. Then the second day, simply have the children print the capital letter alphabet on other papers and hand them in for evaluation and grading.

Lesson 102
Review of Capitals (N–Z)

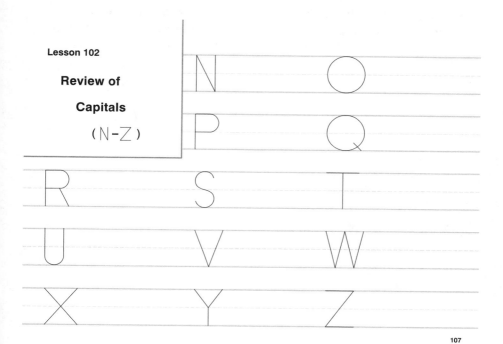

Aim of the Lesson

To review and test the children's understanding of the formation of the last thirteen capital letters of the alphabet.

Directions

The children should trace over each letter and copy it at least twice in the space following.

Conducting the Class

This lesson should be conducted similarly to Lesson 101 unless the alternate suggestion is used as described in the last paragraph of Lesson 101.

Have the children practice the letters on the blackboard. **Briefly discuss them.** At their desks they should **proceed with the lesson** and then **hand it in to you. Evaluate and grade** each child's paper according to the pattern given in Lesson 101.

Unit 5

Writing Sentences

Lessons 103–150

Introduction to Unit 5

As you look at the first lesson in this unit, you will probably notice several things that are different from previous units. One is the lesson format. The other is the decreased letter height.

The full one-inch height was helpful in learning the manuscript letters the first time, since the forms were unfamiliar to the children and they lacked good muscle coordination. The new height is three-fourths inch. This will be the children's first step toward decreased size in handwriting and will help to accommodate the writing of sentences.

This unit concentrates on learning the writing of sentences, but it is actually a review of writing quality as well. Attention will be paid to posture, pencil holding, paper placement, spacing, letter height, and alignment. It will be somewhat easier for you to help our students' writing quality now that they have completed the original learning of the letters.

In addition to emphasizing sentence writing and quality, you will also want to be working on perfecting the children's letter forms. All the small and capital letters will be reviewed. Take advantage of this opportunity to reinforce the formation of the letters. Remember to benefit by the lines provided for extra practice on the back of each student page.

The directions for each lesson will be identified with an asterisk (*).

You will find the teacher's comments not quite as detailed as previously. Greater detail in explanation was necessary in the original learning because of the necessity of establishing a good foundation. Since this unit is basically review, that detailed explanation is not necessary, except as reminders. Rather, the teacher needs to help each child improve the areas of quality and form where he may be lacking.

However, this fact should *not* be used as an excuse for *neglecting* handwriting. As you are aware, the learning process is to continue, following the initial learning. Because this unit is to clinch the work in other units, it should be considered of equal importance with the rest of the units.

Lesson 103
Spacing Between Words
in a Sentence

God is good to us.

God is good to us.

5

Aim of the Lesson

To help the children adjust their writing to a reduced scale; to introduce the children to sentence writing and correct spacing between words in a sentence.

Instructions for the Teacher

At the beginning of the class period, explain to the children that **from now until the end of the year, they are going to be learning to write sentences correctly.**

As the children look at the lesson, **ask them whether they can see anything that looks different** in comparison to other lessons.

273

They may notice that **the letters are smaller** or that **there are six rows on the page** instead of four or five.

Discuss the reduced letter size first. Explain to them that the letters are still made exactly the same as they have been making them, only they are a little smaller.

Next discuss the spacing of words in a sentence. Demonstrate on the blackboard to the children that **the spaces between the words should be the same as the width of the capital letter** *W*. Looking in the book at the sentence "God is good to us," show them how dotted capital *W*'s are used in row one to space between the words. By looking at row two, where the capital *W*'s are left out, we can see that all the spaces are the same and look just right.

*Have the children trace over the sentence each time** in the first two rows and **then copy it four times** in the last four rows.

Work especially on the children's spacing between words, and **watch how well they are adjusting to the reduced letter size.**

Lesson 104
Writing Sentences Using A

Lesson 104   **Writing Sentences Using** A

Adam was made from

dust.

7

Aim of the Lesson

To help each child improve his ability to write sentences neatly and correctly, with emphasis on the letter *A* and spacing.

Instructions for the Teacher

Send the children to the blackboard to review the letter *A*, both small and capital. **Have them give the stroke formation** for each.

*The sentence "Adam was made from dust" should be copied twice on the lines below the sentence. In the empty space beyond the line at the bottom, the same sentence should be copied again.

The children's final copy will be the most accurate test of spacing since the children cannot get spacing help as easily from the printed words.

The main purpose of the use of the letter *W* is to give the children a general idea of proper spacing between words. Explain to the children that a letter cannot always be put between each word in a sentence, for it would be confusing. So **they will need to imagine the width of the letter *W* when they are spacing between words. They should also be careful to make all the spaces equal.** As they finish each sentence, have them look back at their work and see how their spaces look.

Begin working to correct any problems that any child may have in any area of **manuscript writing.** Help each child individually. **Set a goal of having each problem corrected at least by the end of the unit.** By the end of the year each first grader's manuscript handwriting should be as nearly top quality as possible.

Lesson 105
Writing Sentences Using B

Lesson 105   Writing Sentences Using B

The Bible is the best

book.

9

Aim of the Lesson

To help each child improve his ability to write sentences neatly and correctly, with emphasis on the letter *B*, spacing, and adjustment to decreased letter size.

Instructions for the Teacher

Send the children to the blackboard. Have them write the word *Bible* several times, one right after the other, on lines that you have drawn for them. Explain that you want them to space the words correctly, leaving enough space between each word to fit in a capital letter *W*. **Check for spacing errors, and have the children erase**

277

and write over again any improperly spaced words.

While the children are working at the board, **check also how well each small and capital letter** *B* **is being made. Discuss briefly the stoke formation** of both the small and capital letter *B,* and then have the children return to their seats to **proceed with the lesson.**

*In this lesson, the sentence "The Bible is the best book" should be copied twice on the lines below the sentence. In the empty space beyond the line at the bottom, the same sentence should be copied again.

Check carefully for spacing problems, especially in the final copy of the sentence.

How well are the children adjusting to the decreased letter size? For example, has their spacing between letters within a word decreased automatically in proportion to the reduction of height?

Lesson 106
Writing Sentences Using C

Lesson 106   **Writing Sentences Using** C

Christ can do all

things.

11

Aim of the Lesson

To help each child improve his ability to write sentences neatly and correctly, with emphasis on the letter *C*, spacing, and posture.

Instructions for the Teacher

Look with the children at the sentence in the lesson, "Christ can do all things." **Ask them several questions about the content of the sentence.**

Review the formation of the letter *C*. Ask the children, "What is the stroke that makes both the small and capital letter C?" (The curve.)

At the blackboard, **the children should print one or two of both the capital and small letter** *C* on lines that you have drawn for them.

Also on the blackboard, **have them write the sentence "What can Christ do?"** Again, you should emphasize spacing. You may need to help them with spelling if they do not have the words to look at.

Back at their seats **they should proceed with the lesson.**

*Have the children copy the sentence "Christ can do all things" three times, twice on the lines directly below the sentence and once following the vertical line, as in the two previous lessons.

Pay special attention to these areas of your children's writing in this lesson: **the formation of the letter** *C*, **spacing, pencil holding, and posture.**

Lesson 107
Writing Sentences Using D

David did what was

right.

13

Aim of the Lesson

To help each child improve his ability to write sentences neatly and correctly, with emphasis on the letter *D* and period spacing.

Instructions for the Teacher

Review the formation of the letter *D* with the children. Draw their attention to the strokes of both the small and capital letters.

On the blackboard, **have the children print the words *David did* several times. **Each time they should try to make their work an improvement** over the previous time. If there is time, give a counting drill on the small letter *d*.

281

Looking at **the sentence in the lesson, briefly discuss** the fact that David in the Bible was a good man, one who did what was right and loved the Lord with all his heart. We need to be like David.

Draw the children's attention to the period at the end of the sentence. They should already know that a period ends a sentence. But show them where the period is to be placed. Try to help them not to place the period either too close to the word or too far away.

*Have the children copy the sentence "David did what was right" twice on the lines directly below the sentence. In the space following the vertical line, have them copy the sentence a third time; or, as a variation, have the children make up a sentence of their own containing at least one letter *d* and at least four simple words.

Lesson 108
Writing Sentences Using E

Lesson 108   **Writing Sentences Using** E

Each should do his

best.

15

Aim of the Lesson

To help each child improve his ability to write sentences neatly and correctly, with emphasis on the letter *E* and word, letter, and period spacing.

Instructions for the Teacher

Begin the class period by **having a review of the strokes of both the small and capital forms of the letter *E*.** At the blackboard, the children should be given a counting drill on the small form of the letter *e*.

After the children are back at their seats, **talk briefly about the**

283

sentence "Each should do his best." Discuss what doing your best does and does not mean.

Before the children do the lesson, **remind them to space their words and letters the right distance apart.** Also **draw their attention again to the period** and where it is to be placed.

*Have the children copy the sentence twice on the lines directly below. In the space following the vertical line, have them copy the sentence a third time or have them make up one of their own containing the letter *E*.

Watch the children's work especially for poor formation of the letter *E* **and also for improper spacing of words, letters, and the period.**

Lesson 109
Writing Sentences Using F

Lesson 109   Writing Sentences Using F

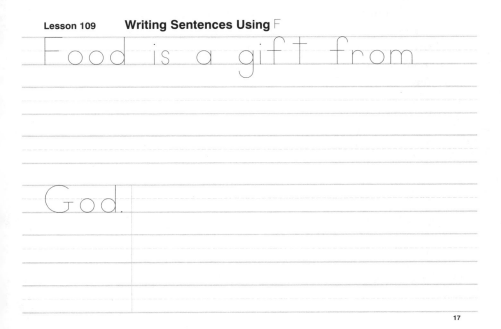

17

Aim of the Lesson

To help each child improve his ability to write sentences neatly and correctly, with emphasis on the letter *F* and crossed-letter spacing.

Instructions for the Teacher

Look with the children at the sentence in the lesson, "Food is a gift from God." Discuss it briefly.

At the blackboard, the children should print the words *Food* **and** *from.* **Discuss the formation of both the capital and small letter** *F*.

*The children should copy the sentence "Food is a gift from God"

285

twice on the lines directly below. In the remaining space, the children should either make another copy of the given sentence or one of their own, containing the letter *F*.

When they make the stem of **the small *f*, be sure that they leave room for the cross on the letter** so that the spacing is accurate.

Especially **watch the children's spacing of the word** *gift*. The *f* and *t* both have crosses and should not be crowded together. The words *gift* and *from* also may be brought too close together because of the cross on the *t* in *gift* and on the *f* in *from*.

How are your left-handed students managing by now? Are they holding their pencils naturally with a straight wrist, or are some developing a hooked wrist?

Lesson 110
Writing Sentences Using G

Lesson 110   **Writing Sentences Using** G

God is good to all

men.

19

Aim of the Lesson

To help each child improve his ability to write sentences neatly and correctly, with emphasis on the letter *G*, posture, word and letter spacing, and adjustment to decrease in letter size.

Instructions for the Teacher

Discuss briefly the sentence "God is good to all men." God is good to all men because He gives rain, sunshine, food, clothing, and so forth. However, not all men appreciate what God is doing for them. They do not thank Him or pay any attention to Him. God wants us to think about how good He has been to us.

Go over the stroke formation of both small and capital forms of the letter *G* with the children.

At the blackboard, **the children should write the words** *God is good*. Help them with spacing and formation in these words where necessary. Especially emphasize the form of capital *G*. Be sure they write each part correctly.

While the children are working at the board, watch their posture. Are they standing up straight, neither too close to nor too far away from the board? How are they holding their chalk?

*At their seats the children should copy the sentence "God is good to all men" twice on the lines immediately below. In the space following the vertical line, have the children copy the sentence a third time or make one of their own containing the letter *G* either small or capital.

Again **reinforce proper word and letter spacing by emphasizing it as the children are doing the lesson.**

By this time the children **should have made a good adjustment to the decrease in letter size.** If any have not, now is the time to help them with spacing, letter form, or any other problems they may have as a result of the change.

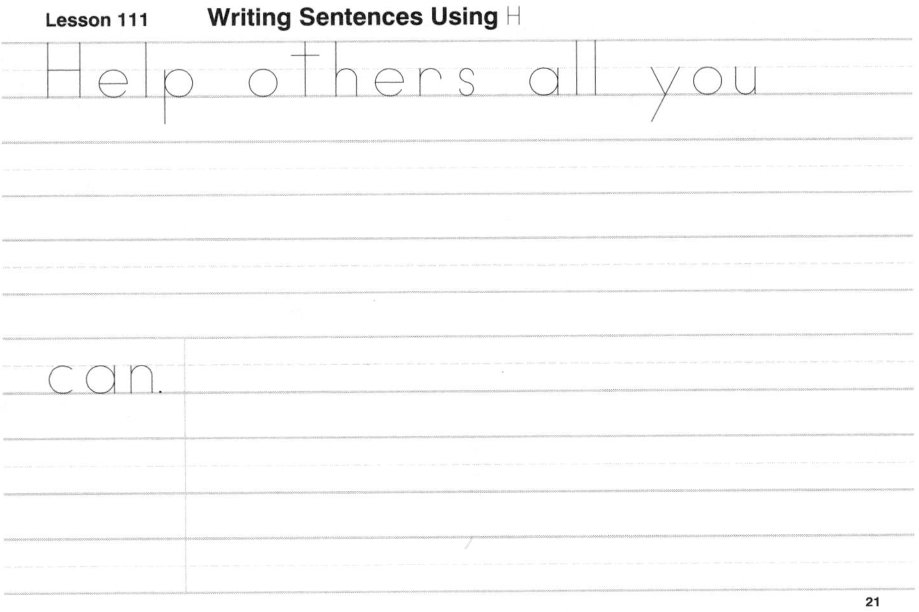

Lesson 111
Writing Sentences Using H

Lesson 111 Writing Sentences Using H

Help others all you

can.

21

Aim of the Lesson

To help each child improve his ability to write sentences neatly and correctly, with emphasis on the letter *H* and circle formation.

Instructions for the Teacher

Send the children to the blackboard. Have them write the words *Help others* **several times.** As they do so, **check on the formation of their capital and small** *H*'s. The letter *H* is fairly simple to make and frequently used, so by this time the children should be making it quite accurately. **Give general instruction and correction** as you see it is needed.

When the children are back at their seats, **look at the sentence** for today's lesson. Discuss briefly ways that children can help their parents, teachers, neighbors, friends, and others.

*Have the children copy the sentence "Help others all you can" twice on the lines directly below. In the space following the vertical line, the children should either copy the sentence a third time or make up one of their own, using a capital or small letter *H*.

There are a number of **small circles and near-circles** in today's sentence. **Are the children making them smoothly and accurately?** You may want to draw their attention to how they are making their circles, especially if there has been any degeneration of form through carelessness.

Lesson 112
Writing Sentences Using I

Lesson 112   **Writing Sentences Using** I

I want to read the

Bible.

23

Aim of the Lesson

To help the children improve their ability to write sentences neatly and correctly, with emphasis on the letter *I* and down-line formation.

Instructions for the Teacher

Discuss briefly the formation of the letter *I*. Put the small and capital forms on the blackboard. Review the letter by drawing attention to the across lines at the top and bottom of the capital *I* and the dot above the small *i*, which is missing from the capital *I*.

At the blackboard the children should print the sentence "I love the Bible." Emphasize getting the down lines on both

the small and capital *I* **straight up and down,** not slanted. Also emphasize making them **as smooth as possible,** without wiggles or zigzags in the line.

Have the children look with you at the lesson. **Discuss the sentence** "I want to read the Bible." Explain simply that one of the reasons that they are learning to read in school is so that they will be able to read the Bible. Even though they are not reading directly from the Bible in their reading books, they are learning words that will make it easier for them to read the Bible.

*The children should copy the sentence "I want to read the Bible" twice on the lines directly below. In the space following the vertical line, have them write the sentence a third time or one of their own containing the letter *I*, either small or capital.

Lesson 113
Writing Sentences Using J

Lesson 113   **Writing Sentences Using** J

Jesus can give joy to

all.

25

Aim of the Lesson

To help each child improve his ability to write sentences neatly and correctly, with emphasis on the letter *J*, alignment, spacing, and formation.

Instructions for the Teacher

Send the children to the blackboard. Have them print the small and capital forms of the letter *J*. After briefly discussing their formation, **have the children print the sentence "Jesus gives joy."**

Ask the children this question about the sentence "Jesus can

293

give joy to all": "Why is it then that not everyone is happy and joyful?" (Many people are not serving Jesus, and that is why they are not happy. They do not let Jesus give them joy.)

In this class period, **make it a special point to emphasize alignment.** Explain to the children the importance of being sure that all the letters touch yet do not overlap the lines that they are supposed to touch. You might want to illustrate correct and incorrect alignment on the blackboard. This: (⫶a⫶) not this (⫶ɑ⫶) or this (⫶ɑ⫶).

*The children should copy the sentence "Jesus can give joy to all" twice on the lines immediately below. After the vertical line, the children can either print the sentence again or write one of their own.

As the children work the lesson, give individual help as you see each child needs it. Again **check spacing carefully.** Smooth and neat letter formation of all the letters is also important

Lesson 114
Writing Sentences Using K

Kind words can cheer

The sick.

27

Aim of the Lesson

To help each child improve his ability to write sentences neatly and correctly, with emphasis on the letter *K*, alignment, and spacing.

Instructions for the Teacher

Discuss with the children briefly **what it is like to be sick.** Sick people cannot do what other people can do. They may have to stay in bed a long time, and they often get very lonely. They like to have people come and speak kindly to them. Sometimes they may especially like to have children visit them to cheer them up. Children should try to be friendly to sick people.

At the blackboard the children should print the words *Kind* **and** *sick*. Note whether they remember just how to place the three strokes of the letter *K* in relation to each other. You might need to help them with this.

*The children should copy the sentence "Kind words can cheer the sick" twice. In the space following the vertical line, they can copy the words *Kind, words,* and *sick* from the sentence.

Remind the children that **their letters should be touching the lines,** as was discussed in the last lesson. Redemonstrate if necessary. **Watch the spacing** of letters, words, and the period at the end of the sentence. **Give individual instruction** as you see each child needs it. Call the class's attention to any error that is being made by a number of students.

Lesson 115
Writing Sentences Using L

The Lord loves all

that obey Him.

29

Aim of the Lesson

To help the children learn to write sentences neatly and correctly, with emphasis on the letter *L*, straight lines, and posture.

Instructions for the Teacher

Send the children to the blackboard. Have the children write the capital and small letter *L* **several times,** very briefly **discussing their formation.** Then **have them print the sentence "The Lord loves us." Check their blackboard posture.** They should be standing straight on both feet, a short distance back from the board.

Discuss the meaning of the sentence "The Lord loves all that

297

obey Him." The Lord has a special love for those who obey Him, or *do* what He says. The Lord loves the people who disobey Him too, but He does not love the bad things they do. He wants them to stop doing bad things so that He will not have to punish them.

*Have the children copy the sentence "The Lord loves all that obey Him" twice on the lines directly below the sentence.

Be sure that the children make their lines straight in forming both the small and capital letter *L*. **Watch their spacing immediately following capital** *L*. The next letter may tend to get too close to it because of the shape of the letter *L*.

Remind the children of their posture as they do the lesson. They should be sitting against the back of their seats, leaning slightly forward from the hips, with both feet on the floor and both arms on the desk.

Lesson 116
Writing Sentences Using M

Lesson 116   Writing Sentences Using M

My mother and father

love me.

31

Aim of the Lesson

To help each child improve his ability to write sentences neatly and correctly, with emphasis on the letter *M* and pencil-holding habits.

Instructions for the Teacher

Talk to the children about how thankful they should be to have parents who love them. Explain that God has given them parents to see to it that they have all the things that they need to live, such as food, houses, and clothing, and to help them when they are hurt or frightened. Most of all, Christian parents help their children to understand the Bible and to do what is right. (If there are children from broken homes in class, you will want to handle the subject with discretion.)

At the blackboard the children should copy the words *My mother,* **and** *me* **twice,** spacing them in sentences form. **Help them especially with small or capital letter** *M* **formation** if you see that any are making either form incorrectly. Also correct other important errors in either form or quality as you see them.

*At their seats the children should copy the sentence "My mother and father love me" twice on the lines directly below. In the space following the vertical line, the children can practice the capital and small letter *M*.

Today **pay attention to the children's pencil-holding habits.** Are they still holding their pencils correctly as they were taught? Go around and **check each child** in this area. They should be holding the pencil loosely, not pinched tightly, and back some distance from the point of the pencil. **You may want to redemonstrate how the pencil is to be held.** Refer to "Posture, Pencil Holding, and Paper Placement" in the introduction to this book.

Lesson 117
Writing Sentences Using N

Lesson 117   Writing Sentences Using N

No one can sin and

get by.

33

Aim of the Lesson

To help the children improve their ability to write sentences neatly and correctly, with emphasis on the letter *N* and accurate and consistent word spacing.

Instructions for the Teacher

Discuss briefly the letter formation of the capital and small letter *N*. At the blackboard **the children should print the words** *No one can* several times. Emphasize the formation of both forms of *N*.

When the children are back at their seats, **discuss the meaning of the sentence** in the lesson. Explain to the children that they should never try to get by, by doing something they know is wrong. Even though their parents or teacher may not find out, God can see everything.

*Have the children copy the sentence "No one can sin and get by" twice on the lines directly below. Following the vertical line, they can write the sentence a third time or use one of their own making.

As you will notice, **there are four small letter *n*'s** in the sentence in the lesson. This is a good time to **check for consistency of formation.** Can the children make each copy of the letter basically the same as all others of the same letter? There may be a little variation but not too much.

Check for accuracy in word spacing again in this lesson. **Check also for consistency in word spacing.** Is each space of equal length? You can do this quite well in today's lesson because of the greater number of spaces between words, as compared with some lessons.

Lesson 118
Writing Sentences Using O

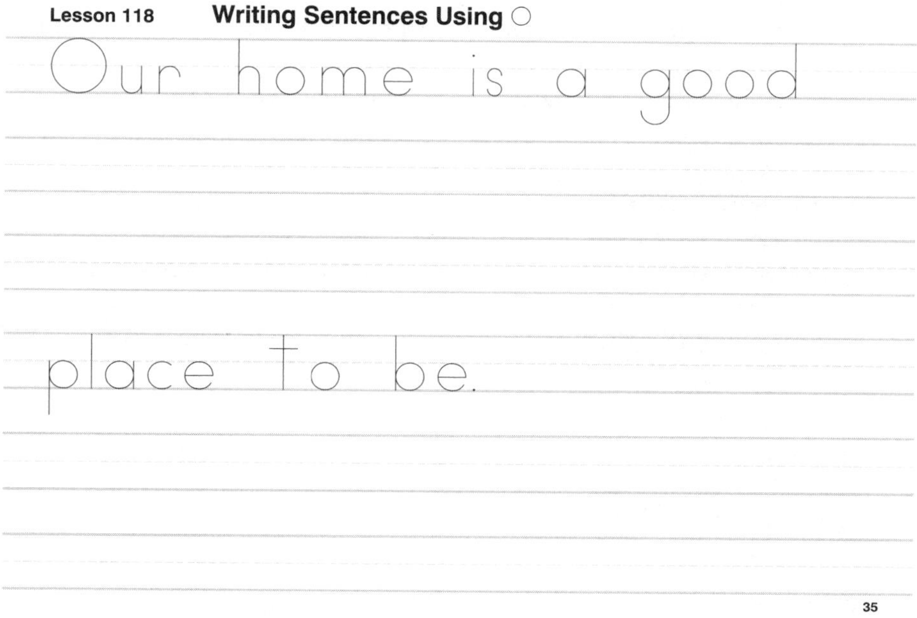

Lesson 118   **Writing Sentences Using** ○

Our home is a good

place to be.

35

Aim of the Lesson

To help the children learn to write sentences neatly and correctly, with emphasis on the letter *O* and quality circles.

Instructions for the Teacher

Your main goal in this lesson will be to **help the children perfect their circles.** Likely none of your first graders make a perfect circle yet (probably even you do not) and can stand some improvement. At the blackboard, they should draw a number of large circles (capital *O*'s) and small circles (small *o*'s) on lines that you have drawn for them. Help them to make the circles as nearly perfect as they are able. Do not push the children so hard in this that they become frustrated, but give as much positive direction as they are able to absorb. **Help them to keep a continuous, even curve all the way around.** As they are drawing the circle, **instruct them to keep looking ahead to see where they are going and then draw there.** If their circles are too wide, too narrow, uneven, jerky, or poorly joined at the closing point, tell them exactly what they should improve. And do not forget to encourage them when they do improve!

After some **practice at the board,** the children should return to their seats. **Look at the sentence in the lesson** with them. Children need to learn to appreciate, even when they are young, that home is to be an enjoyable place. Explain that they can help to make their homes pleasant places to be, by being pleasant themselves.

*Have the children proceed with the lesson by printing the sentence twice on the lines directly below.

Train your eye to be able to pick out writing errors at first glance. Watch the children's work in each area of quality and form, but especially help them with their circle formation if necessary.

Lesson 119
Writing Sentences Using P

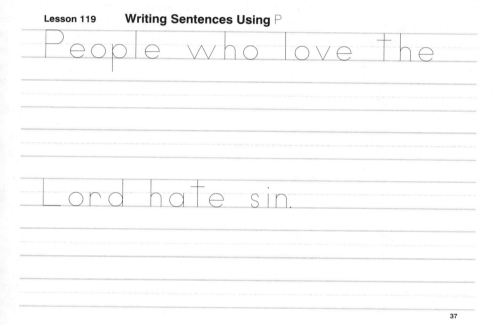

People who love the

Lord hate sin.

37

Aim of the Lesson

To help the children improve their ability to write sentences, with emphasis on the letter *P*.

Instructions for the Teacher

At the blackboard, the children should print the capital *P* and the small *p* several times. Check carefully for inaccuracies in the formation of either form of the letter. Discuss and correct these errors. **For letter-spacing practice** with both forms of *P*, **have them write the word** *People* two or three times.

After the children have returned to their seats, **look at the**

305

sentence with them. Explain that if a person really loves the Lord, he will not like to sin and he will not like to see other people sinning either. That does not mean that he hates the people who do bad things, but he will not like the bad things they do. He might tell people who are doing bad things to stop doing them.

*Have the children proceed with the lesson, copying the sentence two times on the lines below.

As they do the lesson, check the period spacing as well as general spacing between words. They should daily be improving in their ability to get the words spaced consistently

Lesson 120
Writing Sentences Using Q

Quit lying quickly.

39

Aim of the Lesson

To help the children improve their ability to write sentences, with emphasis on the letter Q.

Instructions for the Teacher

At the blackboard, the children should print the capital and small form of the letter Q **several times. Discuss the formation** of each. **Have them also print the sentence "Quit quickly"** as a spacing exercise with the letter Q.

If desired, a counting drill may be given on the small q. This is a one-two count letter (the circle on the first count, the down line and curve on the second count). Demonstrate several times before having your children do it. Then give them about ten letters in a row.

Discuss the sentence in the lesson, "Quit lying quickly." Ask the children why it is important not to lie. Several reasons are, it is not right to make others believe something that is not true; it is disobeying their parents who have told them not to lie; it also is disobeying the Bible, which says, "Lie not one to another."

Remind the children as they begin the lesson **to be sure that each letter is made right and each one just touches the lines** it is supposed to touch. Check carefully for **alignment errors** as the children do the lesson.

*The children should copy the sentence "Quit lying quickly" five times on the lines directly below.

Check your left-handed students again. Are they maintaining the right kind of arm- and hand-positioning habits that you have tried to teach them? If some are not, gently help them to do it correctly, as this is very important (review "Special Instruction for Left-handed Pupils" for general principles).

Lesson 121
Writing Sentences Using R

Lesson 121   **Writing Sentences Using** R

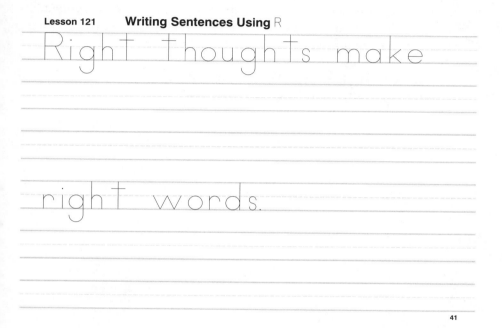

Right thoughts make

right words.

41

Aim of the Lesson

To help the children learn to write sentences neatly and correctly, with emphasis on the letter *R* and crossed-letter spacing.

Instructions for the Teacher

Call attention to the sentence in the lesson, "Right thoughts make right words." Explain to the children that the things we think about are often the things that we say. If we think hateful thoughts, then hateful words will probably come out of our mouths. We need to think kind things about others so that we will say kind things to others and about others.

309

Following this introduction, **send the children to the blackboard. Review the formation of the two forms of the letter** R. **Then have them print "Right words"** twice on lines that you have drawn for them (be sure the first R is capital). **Check spacing around the capital and small** R and between the two words.

In this lesson **call the children's attention again to the spacing of crossed letters.** By using the word *thoughts,* demonstrate on the blackboard how the letter t **should and should not be spaced.** Explain that with the letter t they will need to leave some extra space for the cross since it sticks out on both sides. This is correct: (thoughts); not this: (th o ug hts).

*The children should copy the sentence "Right thoughts make right words" twice on the lines directly below.

310

Lesson 122
Writing Sentences Using S

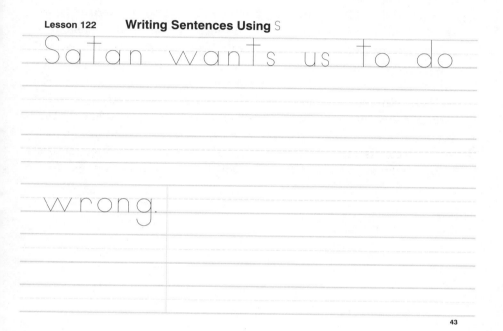

Satan wants us to do

wrong.

43

Aim of the Lesson

To help each child improve his ability to write sentences neatly and correctly, with emphasis on the letter *S* and manuscript strokes.

Instructions for the Teacher

At the beginning of this class period, **give the children a short manuscript stroke review at the blackboard** (to refresh yourself, look back at Lessons 8 and 9). Ask the children to give you the names of as many manuscript strokes as they can. As each is mentioned, have the children print it on the blackboard.

Also **give a brief letter *S* review.** Discuss the fact that the letter

S is made up of two curves going in opposite directions (a double curve). Your children will probably still find that it is difficult to get the two curves to curve and blend just right. Be patient with them as they draw practice letters on the board. **Remind them to use a continuous motion when making the letter,** rather than going "steady by jerks." Gently help them to make corrections when their letters fall short of what they should be.

After the children return to their seats, **look at the sentence in the lesson.** Remind them of the sentence from several lessons previous. "No one can sin and get by." Satan wants us to do what is wrong anyway, even though he knows we will not be able to get by with it. Satan is our enemy, and he does not want us to do what is right.

*The children should copy the sentence "Satan wants us to do wrong" twice on the lines directly below. In the space following the vertical line, they should make two copies each of the manuscript strokes, consisting of twelve strokes altogether: down lines, across lines, backward-slanting lines, forward-slanting lines, circles, and curves.

Lesson 123
Writing Sentences Using T

Lesson 123   Writing Sentences Using T

Try to use your

time well.

45

Aim of the Lesson

To help the children improve their ability to write sentences neatly and carefully, with emphasis on the letter *T* and curve formation.

Instructions for the Teacher

Send the children to the blackboard. Give a short review of the letter *T*, both small and capital forms. **Emphasize making down lines and across lines straight,** without tilting or slanting them. **Then have them print "Time to go" twice. Check for spacing** around the letter *T* and between words.

Discuss the sentence in the lesson, "Try to use your time well."

313

Explain that God has given us time to use, and He wants us to use it the best we can. Sometimes children do not use their time as well as they could. In school, sitting and doing nothing or reading a library book when they should be doing their work is not using their time well. At home, going out to play when they know Father or Mother wants them to help is also not using their time well.

After the children go to their seats, **draw their attention to the curved letters in the lesson sentence.** Have them point these out to you. They are *r, u, s,* and *m.* Demonstrate on the board how the curves of all these letters can be made neatly and smoothly. As the children work, **watch their curves closely. Try to help them make accurate ones** for all four letters mentioned above. Also keep an eye on their **word and letter spacing** and on **proper formation of the letter** *T.*

*Have the children copy the sentence "Try to use your time well" twice on the lines directly below.

Lesson 124
Writing Sentences Using U

Lesson 124 **Writing Sentences Using** U

Under the ground.

God makes food.

47

Aim of the Lesson

To help the children improve the writing of their sentences, with emphasis on the letter *U* and alignment.

Instructions for the Teacher

At the blackboard, you should review with the children the small and capital letter *U*. Also call the children's attention again to the **comparison between small** *u* **and small** *n*. As had been noticed earlier this year, they have exactly the same strokes, only they are inverted.

Following your demonstrations at the board, **have the children**

315

come up. **They should practice both forms of** *U* **several times and write the words** *Under* **and** *ground* at least twice. **Check both spacing and formation.**

Discuss the sentence "Under the ground, God makes food." Ask the children if they know how God makes food under the ground. This time of year, planting has begun, or will soon begin, in many localities. Talk briefly about the kinds of food that grow under the ground, such as potatoes, radishes, carrots, and turnips.

Discuss the comma in this sentence and how it is spaced in relation to the word next to it. **It is spaced the same distance as the period** from the word that it follows. **The space between a comma and the next word would be the width of the letter** *W* the same as regular spacing between words.

*Have the children copy the sentence of the lesson, "Under the ground, God makes food," twice on the lines directly below.

As the children work the lesson, evaluate their alignment. Be sure that it is correct for each letter.

Lesson 125
Writing Sentences Using V

Lesson 125   **Writing Sentences Using** ∨

Very often we love

To pray.

49

Aim of the Lesson

To help the children improve their writing of sentences, with emphasis on the letter *V*, slants, and crossed-letter spacing.

Instructions for the Teacher

As you **look at the sentence** in the lesson, ask the children to tell you some times when they pray. (In family devotions, before meals, in school devotions, at church.)

Have the children pick out **the capital and small V** in the sentence. **Ask two children to** come to the blackboard and **draw the two forms of the letter;** then have the class discuss whether they

317

made them correctly. Emphasize that in making the letter *V,* **they should try to get both sides of the letter slanted the same.** Some children are inclined to make one slant almost vertical and the other one with a greater than normal slant, giving the letter a lopsided appearance (**V**).

At the blackboard the children should make several of the letter *V,* **both small and capital.** Check their slants.

*Next the children should proceed to work the lesson, copying the sentence "Very often we love to pray" twice on the lines directly below.

Remind the children to space carefully between the *f* **and** *t* **in** *often,* since the two letters are crossed letters. These two letters should not be crowded too close together.

Lesson 126
Writing Sentences Using W

We will write as

neatly as we can.

51

Aim of the Lesson

To help the children learn to write sentences neatly and correctly, with emphasis on the letter *W*.

Instructions for the Teacher

In this lesson again **emphasize the slanting strokes** as in the previous lesson. With the letter *W*, as with the letter *V*, all the slants should be correctly slanted. Also **pay special attention to the alignment of the letter** *W*. The letter *W* has many points that touch lines, which creates a greater possibility for alignment error. Help the children to watch each point of the letter.

319

Emphasize the sentence in the lesson. God wants us to do the very best we can in whatever we do. When we are writing, we should try to write just as neatly as possible, not hastily or carelessly. Tell them that, as their teacher, you also like to see when they are doing their very best work.

At the blackboard, the children should print "We will write" several times.

*At their seats, the children should copy the sentence "We will write as neatly as we can" twice on the lines directly below.

Give the children a brief reminder about **word spacing;** check their **posture and pencil holding.**

Lesson 127
Writing Sentences Using X

Lesson 127   **Writing Sentences Using** $\times$

God made all things

in six days. X X X X X

53

Aim of the Lesson

To help the children learn to write sentences neatly and correctly, with emphasis on the letter *X*, spacing, and formation.

Instructions for the Teacher

Discuss the sentence in the lesson, "God made all things in six days." Ask the children what God did the seventh day after He had made the earth and everything in it (He rested on the seventh day).

At the blackboard the children should print the words *six days* **twice** while you check spacing and formation.

*The children should copy the sentence "God made all things in

321

six days" twice on the lines directly below. After the vertical line, the children should copy the row of capital *X*'s twice.

Make this lesson somewhat general, helping the children wherever they need help. **Emphasize the formation of both the capital and small** *X*. Two things are important in the formation of the letter *X*: **the slanted lines should be correctly slanted,** and **they must cross each other at the right place.** For the small *x*, the crossing point is halfway between the middle and bottom lines; for the capital *X*, it is right on the middle line.

Lesson 128
Writing Sentences Using Y

Lesson 128   **Writing Sentences Using** Y

Yes, you should obey

gladly.

55

Aim of the Lesson

To help the children improve their sentence-writing ability, with emphasis on the letter Y and spacing.

Instructions for the Teacher

Ask one of the children to read the sentence in the lesson. Then ask them, "Why should children obey gladly?" (Children should obey gladly because it is expected by God and is the only way for them to be truly happy. And, also, their parents and teachers know better what is best for them than they do.)

Have two of the children draw the two forms of the letter

323

Y on the blackboard as best they can from memory. **Have the other children look at the letters to see if they are made correctly. Demonstrate correctly both forms** of the letter as you briefly discuss the formation with the children.

At the blackboard the children should write the sentence "You should obey" twice. Check their spacing and letter *Y* formation. Remind them not to leave gaps or overlaps between the strokes at the points where they join.

*Have the children print the sentence "Yes, you should obey gladly" twice on the lines directly below. After the vertical line, have them copy the sentence another time or write one of their own, containing the letter *Y*.

Emphasize proper spacing between words as the children work this lesson. Help them to make every letter the best they can.

Lesson 129
Writing Sentences Using Z

Lesson 129   **Writing Sentences Using** Z

Zebras are often

found in zoos.

57

Aim of the Lesson

To help the children improve their ability to write sentences neatly and correctly, with emphasis on the letter Z.

Instructions for the Teacher

Explain to the children that if they have ever seen a zebra, they probably saw it in a zoo. However, zebras do not live naturally in zoos. God makes zebras grow wild in Africa, across the ocean many miles away. Men brought them from Africa to our zoos.

Review with the children the formation of the letter Z. Discuss the fact that the slanting line is to end at a point directly beneath

325

the beginning of the first stroke. **Demonstrate both forms of the letter on the blackboard,** calling out each stroke as it is made. As you print the letters, remember that the slant of the capital Z is steeper than that of the small form.

At the blackboard, the children are to write the short sentence "Zebras are in zoos" at least once. Check formation and spacing.

*Have the children copy the sentence "Zebras are often found in zoos" twice on the lines directly below.

As the children do their work, **watch for accuracy in general letter formation, alignment, and letter and word spacing.**

Lesson 130
Writing Names

Lesson 130   **Writing Names**

John Allen Smith

Martha Ann Miller

59

Aim of the Lesson

To help each child learn to write his own full name more neatly, as well as the names of others.

Instructions for the Teacher

Send the children to the blackboard. Have each of them print his full name. First graders often tend to get the letters of their names quite out of alignment. This is due to the fact that many times they write their names at the top of papers where there are no lines. As they write their names, check to be sure that their alignment is accurate and that they are staying within the lines.

Remind them to space the words of their names the same distance apart as they space the words in a sentence.

*At their seats they should write their names twice on the first two lines and then copy the names *John Allen Smith* and *Martha Ann Miller* in the space below each name.

You may need to **remind the children that all names begin with capital letters.** Be sure none of them begin any name with a small letter.

Lesson 131
Psalm 95:1

Lesson 131   **Psalm 95:1**

O come, let us sing

unto the Lord.

Psalm 95:1

61

Aim of the Lesson

To help the children space words and letters more independently in sentence writing; to introduce the formation of the colon.

Instructions for the Teacher

You will notice in this lesson and in following lessons that **the sentence is arranged differently on the page.** The arrangement of previous lessons helped the child to develop **proper spacing, but this arrangement will help him to develop the skill more independently. For the first little while, you will need to carefully watch the children's spacing** and help them to be careful and correct.

Also **in these lessons help the children learn to be neat and accurate when writing numerals.** The reference for each verse will be given each time, and you should use this opportunity to reinforce the formation of the numerals.

At the beginning of today's class period, **talk just briefly about the verse** in the lesson, explaining that in this verse the Lord is telling us that we should sing to Him. **At the blackboard, the children should print the portion of the verse "Come, let us sing."** Help them here with spacing.

*In doing the lesson, the children should carefully read over the verse and reference and then copy both on the lines following.

Discuss briefly the formation of the colon. Do not try to discuss all of its uses. Simply say that sometimes it acts a little like a period and that it is also used in Bible references. Show them how it is made, with one dot above the other, centered between the lines.

Lesson 132
Isaiah 12:2

Lesson 132   **Isaiah 12:2**

I will trust, and not
be afraid. Isaiah 12:2

63

Aim of the Lesson

To give instruction in some miscellaneous areas of manuscript writing; to reinforce name writing, alignment, and numeral-formation skills.

Instructions for the Teacher

As a review, use this lesson to reinforce the points emphasized in Lessons 130 and 131.

On the blackboard each child should print his full name at least once. Also **have them write the abbreviated sentence "I will trust."**

As you look at the lesson with the children, **discuss the verse briefly.** Help them to think about what the verse says as they write it.

*The children should copy the verse "I will trust, and not be afraid" and its reference at least once. As they work, help them to space correctly.

Also **keep your eye open for any alignment or formation errors** as the children work the lesson. It may take some effort on your part to help the children remember **how to form the numeral 2 correctly.** Remind them that it is made of a curve, a forward-slanting line, and an across line.

Lesson 133
Matthew 22:37

Lesson 133   **Matthew 22:37**

Thou shalt love the

Lord thy God.

Matthew 22:37

Aim of the Lesson

To give instruction in some miscellaneous areas of manuscript writing; in this lesson, on circles and posture.

Instructions for the Teacher

Draw two sets of lines on the blackboard for each child, one above the other. On the upper set they should print the abbreviated sentence "Love the Lord." After they have finished, look over their work, circle the words, letters, or spaces that were made incorrectly, and **have the children correct each error on the lines directly below.**

Have the children go back to their seats. **Discuss the verse briefly.** Explain that we must love God more than we love anyone or anything else in the whole world, even more than our parents and brothers and sisters.

Call the children's attention to the circles in the letter *o, a,* and *d,* and the part circles in *e* and capital *G.* Challenge them again to make their circles neatly and accurately.

*The children should copy the verse "Thou shalt love the Lord thy God" and its reference once on the lines below the verse.

Check their **posture.**

Lesson 134
Proverbs 11:28

Lesson 134   **Proverbs 11:28**

He that trusteth in

his riches shall fall.

Proverbs 11:28

67

Aim of the Lesson

To give instruction in some miscellaneous areas of manuscript writing; in this lesson, on down lines and tenseness.

Instructions for the Teacher

Look at and discuss the verse in the lesson, "He that trusteth in his riches shall fall." Explain that some people think their money will keep them out of trouble. In this verse, God says that it will not. Ask the children to tell you who they think can keep us out of trouble if money cannot.

Have the children look at the large number of down lines

in the lesson, which are found particularly in *t*'s, *h*'s, and *l*'s. **Remind them to make these lines straight,** not wavy.

At the blackboard the children are to print the abbreviated sentence, "He shall fall."

*At their seats, the children should copy the sentence "He that trusteth in his riches shall fall," with the reference, once on the lines below the sentence.

Watch the children as they are sitting at their desks, working the lesson. **Are they tense as they write?** To do their best work, their bodies should be relaxed. Help those who are tense to loosen up their muscles and do their work in a more relaxed manner. Keep watching the children in the days following, to be sure they learn to relax as a habit.

Lesson 135
Proverbs 30:5

Lesson 135   **Proverbs 30:5**

Every word of God
is pure. Proverbs 30:5

69

Aim of the Lesson

To give instruction in some miscellaneous areas of manuscript writing; in this lesson, on small curves and tenseness.

Instructions for the Teacher

Look at the verse "Every word of God is pure" with the children, and briefly explain it to them. It means that no word in the Bible is wrong or sinful or even unnecessary. God said in the Bible all the things that should have been said, and He left out all the things that would not be good for us to read. We should read the Bible to find out what God wants us to know.

In this lesson, **emphasize the small curves especially.** The small letters *r* and *f* both have small curves. The curve on the *r* is made from back to front, while the curve on the *f* is made from front to back.

With the children at the blackboard, count from one to six aloud as they go back and forth on a curve stroke (like in *r* and *f*). Have them do this several times. **Try to help them to retrace the curve exactly** and to make it as uniform and accurate as possible. Also **have them print the abbreviated sentence "God is pure."**

*At their seats, the children should copy the sentence and reference either once or twice (at your discretion), on the lines below.

Again remind your tense children to relax as they write. Go around the room and help them to do so, if necessary. (This does not mean *slouch*. They should be able to relax and still maintain good posture.)

Lesson 136
Proverbs 17:17

A friend loveth at
all times. Proverbs
17:17

71

Aim of the Lesson

To give instruction in some miscellaneous areas of manuscript writing; in this lesson, on capital letters and tenseness.

Instructions for the Teacher

To begin today's class, **have the children come to the blackboard. Have them print this abbreviated sentence: "A friend loveth." Remind them to space accurately** between the words and letters.

Discuss the verse "A friend loveth at all times." Explain to the children, "One is not a real friend who loves you only when everything

339

is going smoothly. Your parents and teachers are real friends because they love and care for you even when you are hurt and crying."

Call the children's attention to the fact that **the word** *Proverbs,* a book of the Bible, **is capitalized.** Emphasize that **books of the Bible always begin with capital letters.**

*Have the children copy the verse "A friend loveth at all times," with the reference, once on the lines below.

Quietly **observe your children again for relaxation and good posture.** Commend those who are learning to relax well. Help any who still are not relaxed as they should be.

Evaluate the children's work, for general letter formation. They are nearly finished with first grade. Is their manuscript-writing quality good enough that they will be ready to begin preparation for cursive writing in second grade?

Lesson 137
Psalm 100:2

Serve the Lord with gladness. Psalm 100:2

73

Aim of the Lesson

To give the children general practice in manuscript writing, and to give instruction in some miscellaneous areas of manuscript writing.

Instructions for the Teacher

Look with the children at the verse "Serve the Lord with gladness." Discuss briefly how we ought to do the things we should without grumbling. Some people wish they would not have to do the things God wants them to do, so they grumble and complain about them. When we do something for the Lord or for others, we should be glad that we are able to help.

341

Send the children to the blackboard for practice. Today **give them a drill to help bring them all up to an efficient rate of writing.** It should especially help those who have been writing too slowly. It can also help those who tend to write too rapidly and carelessly, by slowing them down somewhat.

Conduct the drill in this manner: **Draw lines for each child to write on. Say the letters of the word** *gladness* **at a measured rate of speed** (start by leaving **two-second intervals** between letters). **The children should write each letter when you say it.** After you have finished the word once, **repeat the letters again at a faster rate and then several more times at still faster rates.** However, do not increase the speed to the point that accuracy suffers.

*At their seats, the children should copy the verse with the reference once or twice.

Lesson 138
Psalm 119:11

Thy word have I hid

in mine heart. Psalm

119:11

75

Aim of the Lesson

To give the children general practice in manuscript writing, and to give instruction in some miscellaneous areas of manuscript writing; in this lesson, on the dot of the letter *i*.

Instructions for the Teacher

At the beginning of today's class, **give the children another blackboard drill** to help improve their rate of writing. **Follow the same method used in yesterday's lesson.** Today use the two words *mine heart* instead of *gladness,* and be sure to say the space between the two words as you give the letters. Use the same rates of speed as

343

in yesterday's drill. Do not push the children to the limit.

After the children return to their sears, **discuss the lesson verse.** Explain that hiding God's Word in our hearts includes memorizing Bible verses.

Demonstrate on the blackboard how the letter *i* is to be dotted. Show one letter that is dotted too faintly and one that is dotted correctly. Remind them to make their dots large and distinct so that the letter will never be mistaken for any other letter.

*Have the children copy the verse "Thy word have I hid in mine heart," with the reference, once on the lines below.

Lesson 139
Genesis 18:14

Lesson 139 **Genesis 18:14**

Is any thing too hard
for the Lord?
Genesis 18:14

Aim of the Lesson

To give the children general practice in manuscript writing, and to give instruction in some miscellaneous areas of manuscript writing; in this lesson, on the question mark.

Instructions for the Teacher

Look at the verse with the children and discuss its meaning. Ask the children if they have ever found anything that was too hard for them to do. Explain that there is nothing too hard for God to do, no matter what it is.

Using the words *any thing,* **give another blackboard drill** in the same manner as in the last two lessons.

After the children return to their seats, **give a demonstration of how to form a question mark properly.** Explain that the question mark consists of a curve line at the top, a down line partway to the bottom line and then a period at the bottom line.

*Have the children copy the verse and reference once on the lines below.

Pay attention to your left-handed children as they work the lesson. They should be writing as easily and smoothly as the rest of your children. If they are not, concentrate attention for the next several days on helping them to do so.

Lesson 140
Amos 5:15

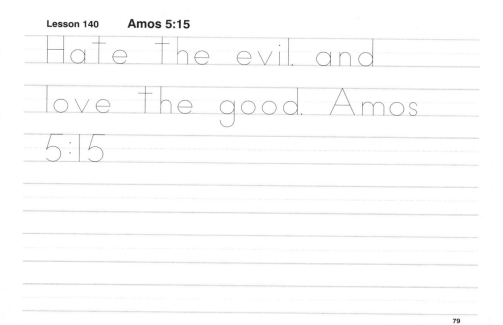

Hate the evil and love the good. Amos 5:15

79

Aim of the Lesson

To give the children general practice in manuscript writing, and to give instruction in some miscellaneous areas of manuscript writing; in this lesson, on commas, circle formation, and *t* spacing.

Instructions for the Teacher

Begin class with a blackboard drill using the words *Love the good*. Again have the children write the letters as you say them at measured rates of speed. Also **have them practice the numeral 5 several times on the blackboard.**

After the children return to their seats, **briefly discuss the**

347

lesson verse. We should not hate people that do evil things, but we should hate the things they do that are bad. We should hate doing bad things ourselves and love to do the things that are good.

*Have the children copy the verse "Hate the evil, and love the good," with the reference, once on the lines below.

As the children work, **remind them to make and space their commas neatly and accurately. Pay attention to their circle formation,** insisting on the maintenance of proper shape. Also **be sure that their letter *t*'s are spaced right** and that the cross is made correctly

Lesson 141
Psalm 118:24

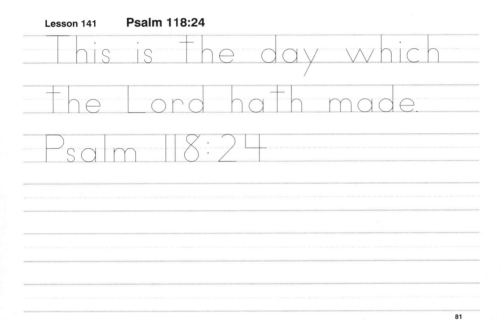

This is the day which
the Lord hath made.
Psalm 118:24

81

Aim of the Lesson

To give the children general practice in manuscript writing, and to give instruction in some miscellaneous areas of manuscript writing; in this lesson, on tenseness and curve formation.

Instructions for Teacher

Begin the class period by **discussing the meaning of the verse** in today's lesson. Explain that God has made each day, which He gives to us each morning. We should want to please the Lord during each day He has given us.

Draw the children's attention to the letters *h, r,* **and** *m.* **All**

349

three of these letters have small curves in the same position. Remind the children that the small curves must be made as smooth and round as possible. **Demonstrate each letter** correctly on the blackboard. **Have the children come to the blackboard and print these three letters** and then the words *This, Lord,* and *made.* Help them with the small curves, and do not be afraid to have them make any letter over, if necessary, in order to get it right.

*At their seats they should copy the sentence "This is the day which the Lord hath made" once, with the reference, on the lines below. Particularly check the curves of the three letters *h, r,* and *m*.

Check again among your pupils for tenseness. Remind them to relax, if necessary.

Lesson 142
Luke 6:28

Lesson 142   Luke 6:28

Bless them that

curse you. Luke 6:28

Aim of the Lesson

To give the children practice in manuscript writing, and to evaluate the children's spacing.

Instructions for the Teacher

In the next several lessons, you should be evaluating the children's progress this year in different areas of handwriting. While you no doubt have been doing this to some degree, do it now with a final grade in mind. While you make this evaluation, **do not forget to consider work that the children have done in other lessons.** Also, the children do not need to know that you are evaluating in any special way.

Take letter grades for each lesson, and keep a record of them for each student.

In this lesson, evaluate the quality of spacing. Check letter spacing (especially crossed letters), word spacing, and period spacing for accuracy and consistency.

Look with the children at the verse in the lesson. Explain that it means we are to speak and act kindly toward those that speak unkindly to us.

At the blackboard the children are to write the same sentence they will write in the book. Give general reminders and corrections as you see the children's writing needs it.

At their seats, the children should copy the verse and reference twice on the lines below.

Lesson 143
Isaiah 55:6

Lesson 143   **Isaiah 55:6**

Seek ye the Lord
while he may be
found. Isaiah 55:6

85

Aim of the Lesson

To give the children general practice in manuscript writing, and to evaluate their work in the areas of alignment and efficiency.

Instructions for the Teacher

Discuss briefly the meaning of today's verse. Explain to the children that God wants people to follow Him when He calls them. If they do not, God might not come to help them when they call for Him.

In this lesson **give the children a rate drill at the blackboard,** using the words *Seek ye the Lord.* Start out the same rate as previously, calling the letters two seconds apart. The following times, increase the rate.

Their performance in a rate drill and their normal writing in doing the lesson will help you to evaluate their efficiency. The question is, **Are the children able to write at an** *efficient* **rate** (not necessarily a *rapid* rate) while also maintaining quality and accuracy in their writing?

You should also be evaluating the children's alignment. Watch the points where the letters should touch the lines. **Make a separate evaluation of rate and alignment.**

*The children should copy the verse "Seek ye the Lord while he may be found" once, with the reference, on the lines below.

Isaiah 45:22

Lesson 144   **Isaiah 45:22**

I am God and there
is none else. Isaiah
45:22

87

Aim of the Lesson

To give the children more reinforcing practice in manuscript writing, and to evaluate the accuracy and consistency of the children's letter formation.

Instructions for the Teacher

Call the children to the **blackboard** for **practice, using the sentence "There is one God."** Give help and reminders wherever you see the children need them.

After the children return to their seats, **discuss today's verse.** Explain that God is talking and is saying that He is the only God.

There are no other real gods, even if people make idols they call gods out of wood and stone.

*Have the children proceed with the lesson. They should copy the verse "I am God, and there is none else" once, with the reference, on the lines below.

Today you should **evaluate both the blackboard work and the lesson work of your children for accuracy and consistency in letter formation.** Look first for accuracy and then for consistency. Are all the lines and circles made neatly and joined together properly?

There are a number of letters in this lesson that are used more than once. **Look at** *a, o, d, n, h, e,* **and** *s* **to be sure the children are making their letters consistently.**

Take one letter grade only for accuracy and consistency in letter formation.

Lesson 145
Proverbs 15:3

Lesson 145   **Proverbs 15:3**

The eyes of the

Lord are in every

place. Proverbs 15:3

Aim of the Lesson

To give the children increased practice in manuscript writing, and to evaluate their posture and pencil-holding habits.

Instructions for the Teacher

At the beginning of class, have the children go to the **blackboard** and **practice, using the sentence "God sees everything."** Have them print it several times.

Briefly explain "The eyes of the Lord are in every place" to the children. Tell them that this means God sees everything and knows when they obey or disobey their parents.

*Have the children copy the verse "The eyes of the Lord are in every place" once, with the reference, on the lines below.

It may seem as though posture is but indirectly related to penmanship. However, it plays a part important enough to be considered in your evaluation. Pencil holding and chalk holding are also important in their relation to good penmanship. If you have been reminding the children frequently in these areas, as suggested in previous lessons, they should be aware of what is expected of them.

When you evaluate the children's posture, pencil-holding, and chalk-holding habits, draw from more than just today's lesson. Keep in mind how they have performed in these areas previously. **Ask these questions about their work:** Do they pinch their pencils? Do they slouch or sit in their seats in some other improper way? Do they slouch or stand too close while working at the blackboard?

Give one letter grade for your evaluation of posture and pencil holding.

Lesson 146
Proverbs 20:11

Lesson 146   **Proverbs 20:11**

Even a child is known
by his doings.
Proverbs 20:11

91

Aim of the Lesson

To give the children more practice in manuscript writing, and to evaluate their ability to write and remember the manuscript strokes.

Instructions for the Teacher

Today give a manuscript-stroke review at the blackboard. Draw each manuscript stroke on the board one at a time, though not in the order in which they were originally learned. Have the children raise their hands if they know the name of the stroke you have made. Then turn the process around. Say the names of the strokes for the children to draw on the blackboard.

Evaluate and grade both the children's recognition of the various strokes and their ability to make the strokes.

Send the children to their seats and then **explain today's verse.** Tell the children that it means that people can tell what kind of children they are by the things they do. For example, if a child does not tell the truth, people know that he is a liar. Older people also are known by the things they do.

*Have the children copy the verse and reference once on the lines below. Give general help and reminders wherever you see they need them.

Lesson 147
Proverbs 14:9

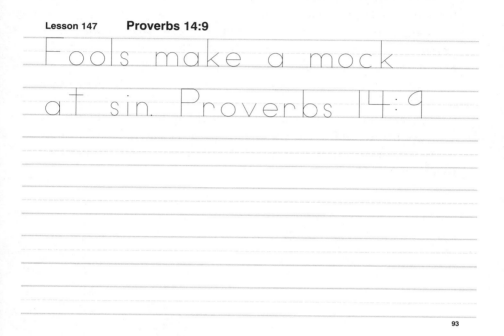

Fools make a mock

at sin. Proverbs 14:9

93

Aim of the Lesson

To give the children more practice in manuscript writing, and to evaluate their numeral formation.

Instructions for the Teacher

At the blackboard **the children should print the ten manuscript numerals** one at a time. **Have a child describe the formation of each numeral aloud** as the other children print them. Be sure he describes them correctly.

Here are several things you should remember as you review numerals with the children:

361

1. The down line on the numeral 5 is slightly forward slanted.
2. The circle on the bottom of the numeral 5 is larger than a small circle, rising above the middle line.
3. The 0 should be one full circle, not made as an oval at this point.
4. The curves of the numeral 3 are greater than half circles.
5. The numeral 9 has a "corner" on one side.

Remind the children of these five points by demonstrating these numerals at the blackboard.

Discuss briefly the meaning of the verse "Fools make a mock at sin." It means that a person is foolish if he thinks he can get by with doing what is wrong, because no one can get by with sin.

*At their seats the children should copy the verse "Fools make a mock at sin," with the reference, once on the following two lines. On the two bottom lines, they should print the numerals from 1 to 10. Pay special attention to the children's numerals, and help them where necessary. **Evaluate their numerals and give a grade on numeral formation.**

Lesson 148
Review of Small Letters

95

Aim of the Lesson

To evaluate the children's formation of small manuscript letters.

Instructions for the Teacher

*At the beginning of this class period, have the children open their books to this lesson. **They should print each small letter in alphabetical order** once on the lines. Remind them to do their best, since they will later need to write each incorrect letter correctly several times.

When all the children have finished the small alphabet on paper, **go over their letters quickly for accuracy and neatness.** Tell

363

the children which letters need improvement and why. **The children who have incorrect letters should go the blackboard and print those letters correctly several times.** Be sure they are not making the same errors on the blackboard as they did on paper.

Look back at Lessons 50 and 51 to help you remember the correct formation for any letter you may have a question about.

Evaluate carefully, without being overly particular. Look for general accuracy in formation, smoothness, and neatness. **Do not take a grade** until you have finished the next lesson, which reviews capital letters.

Lesson 149
Review of Capital Letters

97

Aim of the Lesson

To evaluate the children's formation of manuscript capitals.

Instructions for the Teacher

*Follow the same pattern as in the previous lesson. **Have the children carefully print the manuscript capitals on the lines of the lesson. Check for accuracy** and have the children make each incorrect letter correctly several times on the blackboard.

Check Lessons 101 and 102 if you have any questions on capital letter formation.

Take a grade on your evaluation of the children's formation from this lesson and the previous one.

365

Lesson 150
Final Test

99

Instructions for the Teacher

The following sentences compose **the test:**

This year I have learned to write. God has helped me. I want to thank Him.

The children should print these sentences on the lines of the lesson as you read them orally. **Give a word or two at a time,** spelling words out as necessary. Allow them all the time they need. **Say each period and capital and each space between sentences.** When they are finished, have them give you their papers for grading.

Evaluate and grade the test carefully. Watch for errors in neatness, smoothness, and accuracy in letter formation. Spacing and

366

alignment of letters are also important and should be taken into consideration when evaluating.

To arrive at a final grade for the year, average the grades which you have taken in the last eight lessons. Then find the average of the test grade and that grade.